IF YOU LIKE PIÑA COLADAS...

ounds, for relationship,
ckout on marriage.

ear-old northern celery
t seeks hot tomato for
ed salad; two croutons
ided.

et Valentine candy and
ance is hidden under a
shell, this 40 year old
M will deeply warm your
t and melt in your hand
you can see beyond his
entrepreneurial shell
get to his soft center.

k, mint condition, low
s, good engine. Nice
llights and bumper.

sic '47 Leo, original

GWM wizard ISO
looking for love un
rainbow. I could pr
brain, heart and ne
someone in the fell
mode. You should b
ably intelligent, per
sensitive and finan
dependent. Please
man, tin men or pu
need apply.

Leading lady soug
of lifetime. Scenes
scintillating dialog
dancing, outdoor a
improvisation.

Fair-haired maiden
single WM with th

IF YOU LIKE PIÑA COLADAS...

The Humor and Weirdness of Personal Ads

Al Hoff

Andrews McMeel Publishing
Kansas City

www.andrewsmcmeel.com

99 00 01 02 03 BIN 10 9 8 7 6 5 4 3 2 1

Library of Congress Cataloging-in-Publication Data
Hoff, Al. 1964–
If you like piña coladas— : the humor and weirdness of personal ads / Al Hoff.
p. cm.
ISBN 0-7407-0034-0 (pbk.)
1. Personals—Humor. I. Title.
PN6231.P36H64 1999
646.7'7'0207—dc21 99-21802
CIP

Design and composition by Mauna Eichner

Acknowledgments

I am deeply indebted to the many across the country who sent personal ads for my perusal: Dave Nuttycombe, Candi Strecker, John Marr, Lynn Peril, Jen Hitchcock, Lee Gerstein, Scott Maiko, Brother Randall, Herb Jue, Malcolm Riveria, Rob Elliott, Lance Laurie, Joy Fuqua, Chantal Nadeau, Amy Lavelle, Bruce Townley, Dave Frame, Barbara Kligman, Mary Alice Rosko, Matthew Tinkcom, Matthew Veltkamp, Mike Mueller, Steve Kuhn, Julie Lindemann, Johnie Shimon, Mark Maynard, Craig Mitchell, Teddy Ficklen, Jenny Boe, Mary Driscoll, Kelly Patterson, Betty Maple, Alison Franks, Lara Weigand, Angela Masloff, Karen Isleib, Michael Harwell, Ian Loomis, and Melissa Farron. Thanks to Kim Witherspoon, Christine Schillig, and Jean Zevnik for their work in publishing this collection. Above and beyond the call of duty: Tina Plottel, Michelle Gienow, and, as always, Pat Clark.

Introduction

I've always loved reading the personal ads. I'm captivated by those little blocks of text condensing somebody's life, looks, hobbies, and hopes into four or five lines. It's so few words for the formidable task of selling themselves and hopefully attracting others. Sadly, most advertisers choose to parrot the same predictable, dull ad, but others tackle this restraint with inventiveness or bravado.

The examples and excerpts compiled here represent the oddest and funniest ads I've read—the crazy analogies (I am a car, a bottle of wine, an airplane), the poems, the alliteration, the unfortunate typos, the bizarre requests ("You must possess the qualities of Jesus and Sting combined."), and the curiously described assets ("fattish hair"). These ads have been culled from over

50,000 hilarious and bizarre real personal ads nationwide—ordinary written ads from ordinary papers from ordinary people looking for ordinary relationships.

The goal of the book is not to mock those who use the personals to find relationships but to delight in the rare ads that stand out from the pages of nearly identical ads. I don't know who is placing the ads, who (if anybody) is responding, or how the dates went. I didn't pick these particular ads because I thought they'd be more likely to get a response. I chose them because something about how they were written made them more interesting. If one of these ads is yours, please don't take offense. Rejoice that out of tens of thousands of extrastrength dull ads I read, I noticed yours!

Things to Know

Here is the code to the standard abbreviations used in personal ads.

ISO–In search of

S–Single

M–Male

F–Female

G–Gay

Bi–Bisexual

D–Divorced

WW–Widowed

W–White

B–Black

H–Hispanic

A–Asian

O–Oriental

J–Jewish

P–Professional

NR–Nonreligious

NS, n/s–Nonsmoking

ND, n/d–Nondrugging

LTR–Long-term relationship

VGL–Very good-looking

yo–Years old

#–Pounds

All other mysterious acronyms are courtesy of the individual advertisers. Unless specifically noted, these ads are in their original form. They have not been cut or edited.

LOVE BUGS

Cockroaches fascinate me, as do men who scuttle about passionately on thin legs, investigating time, space, thought, food with dogged determination. This sophisticated, striking, 40-ish, pseudo-entomologist seeks the perfect specimen: tall, dark, wingless but ready to fly.

Queen Bee with share-sting, tired of drones, seeks mate for setting up hive, tending honeycomb, pollinating whatever strikes our fancy, and making some sweet honey.

Honeybee seeks flower. SWM, 36, seeking pretty young SWF, sweetheart. Need your pollen. My sting will keep you blooming.

LOVE BIRDS

Lonesome Dove—Small, smart, savvy swan seeks 50–60-something soaring seagull.

Relearning to Fly. SWPM, 33, single dad. Like Icarus, have flown too close to the sun. ISO Lady Livingston Seagull to help me spread my wings and share the sky.

The Male Bird (DJM, 44 y.o., 5 ft. 9 in./155 lbs., brn/brn) built his nest (N. Arlington) and decorated it (neatly). He's looking for a nice female bird (S/DF, NS, slim, attractive, no chicks in nest). Now he hops and chirps (monogamous, romantic, attentive, gentle, good cook) to attract her (for LTR, billing and cooing).

Hiking, biking, culture vulture seeks "raptorous" relationship with one bright, funny, easy to look at, easy to be with SWM feathered friend (43–55). Habitat includes the outdoors (obviously), theatres, museums, music clubs, restaurants, airports, SW "bird," 5′ 2″, trim, fit, slightly offbeat, slightly wacky frequent flyer wants to share life, love, and the pursuit of happiness. Don't hide in your nest alone; pick up the phone.

MY LITTLE PONY

Horse Power—

SMB, 37, 6′ 4″. Built like a Clydesdale, has a Thoroughbred's grace. Are you ready to saddle up and ride into the sunset?

Frisky purebred filly seeks prancing stallion for frolics in the meadows. Pedigree unimportant, but filly is 18.5 hands overall (6′ 2″) so please be at least 19 hands tall (6′ 4″). My coat is red, eyes are blue. I'm 41, coltless, educated, successful, attractive, height/weight proportionate, healthy.

Beautiful, spirited palomino mare, blue eyes, soft mouth, English, Western, evening dressage. Surefooted. No bad habits, rears if mistreated. Prefers Christian handler, 45–58.

LOVE CATS

Sweet Kittycat diligently searching for intrepid, aggressive male beast who can make me purr. Must be willing to mark and defend territory—just don't scratch the furniture.

Purr-fect!—Single white female, 32, 5′ 1″, 120 lbs., black hair, brown eyes, this playful kitten is declawed and cotton soft. On the prowl for a male lion (not a male line) who's single white male, 5′ 7″+, 25–40. Meeting the cat's meow would be "mewsic" to my ears. Not into cat and mouse games! No fur balls and tuna breath!

ISO Lion King—
SWF, 5′ 4″, blue-eyed, tawny-maned lioness, 36, ISO lion king to inflame, claim, and tame her. Let us rule by day and prowl by night. Loyalty, courage, and humor a must. Erotic and eccentric a plus. Cubs are welcome.

Leo—Sexy lioness back on the prowl. Petite white professional female, 45, nonsmoking brunette beauty searching for lion king. Scratching and biting—all possible. Let's go for a kill, dance all night, hunt all day. Are you male enough to satisfy this lioness? Give me a roar-purr.

OUT IN THE HILLS

12 point buck has seen 42 summers. Looking for doe to settle under the pines with. Leave sign and will rendezvous in cornfield with you.

12 Point Buck Seeks Doe—
Prancer ISO Vixen for reindeer games and more. I'm 25, tall, muscular, and attractive with a shaved head, warm and fuzzy on the inside (but you needn't be). Seeking intelligent, witty doe. No cloven hooves please.

Alaskan-Bushed "Wolf"!— Nocturnal Illusive Petite Howling Bohemian Brunette, 39—Long-Haired Caring Companion with Highly Creative Paws—Would Like to Meet Refined Calm Rustic Empathic Established "Gentlemanly" Wolf (Tall Poetic Loyal Loving . . . Non-smoking, 34–43) for Sailing Kayaking Dining Theatre Symphony Tundra Expeditions!!!!

Wolves Mate for Life—

Lone male wolf seeks female wolf for foraging, romps, and possible howling at the moon. Having a litter of cubs is a definite possibility. 37, 158 lbs., blue eyes, and good coat. Let's rub noses and hold paws.

A beast within—Loyalty, trustworthiness, honesty... these are all things I hold dear to my heart. But more importantly, my instincts. Like the wolf, my totem animal. I have lost many friends to my clad beliefs. Help Lord Wolven find his beauty.

Release the hounds!
Long lean silver fox awaiting capture by spirited thoroughbred. Embraces life, loves people, cats, good food, movies. Excited about what God has in store for us. Come lure me out of my burrow and be ready for an exciting chase!

BARNYARD LOVE

Razorback seeks sow. Let's hook up our curly tails, and I'll rub oinkment all over your pigskin. Potbellied sows need not apply. Your sty or mine.

Old Bull ISO heifer. Fun, fit, 50-ish WM who enjoys grazing in quiet pastures, moo-ving on fast wheels, small furry, four-legged friends. Let's share a bag of oats.

MAN'S BEST FRIEND

Mutt for adoption—healthy coat, frisky, loyal, friendly, affectionate, trim, attractive. Likes outdoors, but good city dweller. Happy disposition. Likes to hump. Responds to rolled paper. Not good around children, otherwise well-behaved. Free to attractive, slim female, under 43.

Dog Catcher Wanted—This dog can be found at the gym, running with the pack, skiing or boarding, climbing mountains, or in the doghouse. Description: 5′ 10″, 185 pounds, brown/blue, 5′ ½″. Remember, dogs are faithful, affectionate, intelligent, forgiving, playful, athletic, and loving. Successful dogcatcher should be over 5′ with medium to slender build. Longer hair and lighter eyes preferred, about 4 to 5 years. No smokers, drugs, or cats.

Show-quality long-haired dog with nice tail and admirable wag of Pointer/Setter mix seeks similar breed to run with. Enjoys a swim, chow, bone burying, and an occasional romp through the neighborhood. Paws off for huskies and poodles.

Free to Good Home—
Handsome Black male, excellent health, had shots, trustworthy, house-trained, does tricks, good with kids. Will not bite exes. Works for food, great protection. Comes with all the accessories, can be delivered to you ASAP. Ready to love only you!

Lost dog seeks owner. Lost, can't find way home. Seeks someone tall, intelligent and creative, liberal and exciting.

If a dog is man's best friend, why go on a fox hunt? It may turn out to be a wild goose chase. SWF, 36, plain but sexy, seeks snake.

ELVIS FANS

"Are You Lonesome Tonight"—"Angel" looking for a "Girl Happy," "Hunk a Hunk a Burning Love," 39–50, "To Kiss Me Quick," "Get Me All Shook Up," so "I Can't Help Falling in Love with You."

Elvis has left the building. Wise Men say that only fools rush in, but since when do people listen to wise men? The SWM, 25, 6′, brown/green, has had A Mess of Blues in my time, but I'm checking out of Heartbreak Hotel and asking anyone: Are You Lonesome Tonight? If you are, Don't Be Cruel and let me be your teddy bear. It's Now or Never, so call. Because now and then, there's A Fool Such As I, but we're rare, endangered. (Hardheaded women need not call this softhearted man.)

DISCO DANCERS

Free & Single—Be the "Flashlight" in my "Disco Inferno"! I am a SF, 22, ISO a "Dr. Boogie" to help me "Turn the Beat Around." Not built like a "Brick House" ("Knock on Wood"); not looking for any sucker MC's or "Superfreaks," just someone who's "Staying Alive." "Let the Music Play!"

I have Night Fever for you. How Deep Is Your Love? Don't give me any Jive Talkin'. [Bee Gees]

Disco Down. I am the original Disco Duck. Quack Quack. Get down mamma! Can you shake your tail feathers?

up with one bright, easy to look at, easy with SWM feathered l (43-55).

blood—This charming 37 seeks the perfect F and new lover with lips ugar: "boy meets girl" God, send me an angel won't tear us apart.

1, colt-less, educated, ssful, attractive, t/weight proportionate ty.

put on our capes and and team up for ad- re! To the Batpoles! s, Two-Faces and Cat n need not apply.

white male seeks ly Baywatch wannabe nows when to turn it ad when to turn it on. red: mouth to mouth citation.

20's woman looking gothic man who has a g for the darker thing

e foundation and al- ve appearance add to ality and charm. Pre- y: you are handsome, 3-41), financially, emo ly and physically fit, appreciate!

ector's item, low mai ce and some assembly ed. Act now, and re- a boomerang demon- n free! Hurry! Offer d.

, 28, tall, slender gs thrown/blue color e). Safe for outdoor hletic use. Many hold uses in garden, hop, kitchen. Travel (extensively field overseas).

ar oldprofessional g for match who's 25 ndsome, honest, ma- nd not looking for rary source of heat

WF, 29, avid swimmer, ag private investigator is fishing for a n who isn't afraid of ep end.

dust off my cover and run her fingers through my pages.

Coach—under 50, conscious, considerate, honest, patient, into snuggling, sailing. Spir- ited at challenging ladies. Call for tryouts.

1949 or 1953. Better like dogs.

Get your hands dirty with this hot young archaeologist looking for an Indiana Jones to excavate my secret pas- sageways. Must have a mind

that glimmering star to cap- ture me in her gravitational pull. One star planet, will orbit you with affection, his molten core will fuel those passions to keep your sparkle shining.

I'm your candidate for

animated cuddlers to hiber- nate with in the 100 Acre Woods of life.

SM interested in meeting an individual who can surprise me with her unique and of- fensive beauties, not her ex-

sense of humor, Wort's strength, Riker's height, Geordi's intelligence and communicator skills like Pi- card. I am shapely like Troi.

Robert DeNiro kinda guy. Seeks woman with Green- wich Village cool. Little

graduate student, 31, Me: postmodern hipster, English- Literature degree, rockabilly, like waffles. You: must hate hippies, drunks, frozen yo- gurt. Cat: black.

Dashing, 31, 6'3", 180lbs,

er former boyfriend! Ne ails! References availab

50 Meaningful relations with cute dyke who can air Ford pick-up truck.

Unmask, join hands, jun down, spin around, plung nto the pool? Ecstatic l porpoises? I say we do it

SWM, 5'10", 200 pound lack hair, eyes. Seeking mail, all redhead, young oney. I want the bubble be coated for us with ho always.

hose men who cuddle whores for love are sedat y their darling's charms only have tired arms fre aving hugged the clouds bove.

On the prowl for a male I not a male line) who's si hite male, 5'7"+, 25-40

SWM, 36, seeking pretty oung SWF, sweetheart. Need your pollen. My sti vill keep you blooming.

Petite white professional male, 45, nonsmoking brunette beauty searchin or lion king. Scratching iting—all possible. Let's or a Fill, dance all night, unt all day.

Rare Violin seeks matchi ow for warm harmoniou encounters. Fretwork in- cludes exceptional curves reen eyes, auburn hair. I strument produces melod us, intelligent, witty sou njoy sharp shifting, ac ostbite. Blood type unli portant. Must like drago pending some evening alone.

User-friendly, software de nized for a romantic, long erm relationship. Proce

ROCKERS

Dr. Love Seeks Christine Sixteen. Don't be a Hard Luck Woman on October 6th. Single white male, 38 yrs., 6 ft. 1 in., 185 lbs., athletic, non-smoker, non-drinker, seeks non-smoker, non-drinker Strutter to set my soul on fire. I want you to attend the Kiss concert. Don't meet me in the ladies room but at the USAir Arena. So shock me and send me your best cute picture to your God of Thunder.

Lizard Kings—I want to be your Lizard Queen. SF ISO Jim Morrison double (A Doors Fan will do) to live on Love Street with.

Help—I need somebody, not just anybody. We'll Follow the Sun down The Long and Winding Road. I Want to Hold Your Hand through Strawberry Fields Forever. DWF, 45, 5′ 5″, 120 lbs., brown-eyed, blond seeks attractive rugged but gentle male. [Beatles]

Crazy Diamond Still Shining On! Wish You Were Here. Are your walls too high to see my shine? If you'll open your eyes and see me, you won't rely on organized deceit. Dashing, 31, 6′ 3″, 180 lbs., blue eyes. You are: 22–30, sincere, nonsmoker, in shape. [Pink Floyd]

ALTERNATIVE MUSIC FANS

Happy When It Rains?—Are you a creep, a weirdo? Have you ever felt stupid and contagious? Are you only happy when it rains? Call me, we'll drown together? Eclectic, tall and thin, open-minded, hazel eyes, humorous, blonde hair, intelligent, professional, cat person.

Love Like Blood—

This charming man 37 seeks the perfect F. A brand new lover with lips like sugar, "boy meets girl," dear God, send me an angel, love won't tear us apart.

Only met 10,000 Maniacs—
43, divorced, trim, 5′ 9″, cute. No Stone Temple Pilot, Sgt. Pepper's Lonely Hearts Club member, U2? I've Got Everything but the Girl. Let's tune together, people'll say They Might Be Giants. No flats, sharps, or sour notes. Just B natural.

COUNTRY TWO-STEPPER

Non-smoker, tired of "Standing Outside the Fire," let's "Meet in the Middle." Seeking SWM, 28–38, non-smoking to "Rock My World" and treat me like the "Queen of Memphis," let's get "Reckless" tonight.

INSTRUMENTS OF LOVE

Rare Violin seeks matching bow for warm harmonious encounters. Fretwork includes exceptional curves, green eyes, auburn hair. Instrument produces melodious, intelligent, witty sound. Bow should be well-rehearsed, educated, and stable, with varied repertoire. 48–60, WASP, non-smoker, about 6′, 180–225.

Stradivarius seeks virtuoso to help this instrument sing. Recently discovered with minor scratches, in good condition. Friendship first, possible LTR.

Let Me Tell You About My Brain

Most people go with the basic terminology like "smart," "intelligent," or "degreed," to illustrate their mental prowess, but a few are specific about their gray matter.

It's a . . .

functional brain
good working brain
fully equipped brain
massive brain
stable brain
powerful brain
engineering brain
big brain
polished brain
class brain
bulging brain
business brain
agile brain
uber-brain
huge brain

I have . . .

smarter brains
East Coast brains
big brains
surplus brains
substantial brains
both sides of brain
a big braincase

I am . . .

right-brained
Pentium-brained
somewhat brainy (Ivy)
mega-brained
well-endowed mentally

I'm smart; I got a . . .

rocket science mind
spacious mind
mind of a stallione [*sic*]
mind of a poet
packed cranium
well-endowed cranium
big giant head

I AM THAT TV SHOW

Underdog seeks Wonder Woman, leash me with your golden lasso; I'll be true. No more saving sweet Polly. Fly me away in your invisible plane.

Speed Racer—Man on the go, seeks Trixie, 21–30, willing to take high risks to cross finish line together. Plenty of adventures and bad dialogue, wants more than just a pit stop.

Ernie Seeks Bert—Fit Bi Filipino guy (28) with Ernie's humor, Kermit's intellect, Grover's charm, and Cookie Monster's appetite seeks fit Bi/GWM (23–30) to spend sunny days chasing the clouds away.

Dynamic Duo—Holy romance! Batman seeks Robin! Let's put on our capes and cowls and team up for adventure! To the Batpoles! Jokers, Two-Faces, and Catwoman need not apply.

SWM, 24, Wile E. Coyote type supergenius: eclectic, creative, and complete with existential angst. You: light-hearted Road Runner type, minus the cruelty, with a smiling appreciation for all my ridiculous schemes. My heart is a giant magnet and for once you actually ate the birdseed full of ball bearings. Bzzt! Clank!

Greg Seeks Marcia—Since we're not really related, I wanted to say I think you're groovy. Let's listen to your funky 8-tracks. I am a 25 SWM with the coolest threads.

Let's Play Jeopardy!—"Smart, humorous, sensual women for 100, Alex." The answer: You. The question: Who responded to the personal of an inventive, upbeat, successful DWM, 46? You won't be in Jeopardy!

Bud Bundy seeks Al Bundy. Late 20s, gay white male, smaller build, goatee, seeking older working-class male for party buddy. Let's sit on the couch, drink beer, and watch sports, wrestling, COPS, and movies. Bisexual smoker/drinker a plus.

ship with one bright,
y, easy to look at, easy
e with SWM feathered
nd (43-55).

e blood—This charming
n 32 seeks the perfect F
rand new lover with lips
sugar, "boy meets girl"
r God, send me an angel
won't tear us apart.

41, coil-less, educated,
cessful, attractive,
ht/weight proportional
thy.

's put on our capes and
is and team up for ad-
ture! To the Batpoles!
ers, Two-Faces and Cat-
nan need not apply.

gle white male seeks
dly Baywatch wannab
knows when to turn it
and when to turn it on.
uired; mouth to mouth
scitation.

ly 20's woman looking
a gothic man who has
ing for the darker thing

gle foundation and at-
tive appearance add to
quality and charm. Pre
ify: you are handsome,
33-41, financially, emo
ally and physically fit,
to appreciate!

ollector's item, low mil
ince and some assembl
uired. Act now, and re-
e a boomerang demon-
tion free! Hurry! Offer
ed.

M, 28, tall, slender
ngs (brown/blue color
me). Safe for outdoor
athletic use. Many
sehold uses in garden,
kshop, kitchen. Travel
y (extensively field
d overseas).

ear old professional
ing for match who's 25
handsome, honest, ma-
and not fool ing for
porary source of heat

GWF, 29, avid swimm
ling private investigato
er, is fishing for a
an who isn't afraid of
deep end.

dust off my cover and run
her fingers through my
pages.

Coach—under 50, conscious,
considerate, honest, patient,
into snuggling, sailing. Spirited at challenging ladies.
Call for tryouts.

1949 or 1953. Better like
dogs.

Get your hands dirty with
this hot young archaeologist
looking for an Indiana Jones
to excavate my secret pas-
sageways. Must have a mind

that glimmering star to capture me in her gravitational
pull. One star planet, will
orbit you with affection, his
molten core will fuel those
passions to keep your
sparkle shining.

I'm your candidate for

animated cuddlers to hiber
nate with in the 100 Acre
Woods of life.

SM interested in meeting an
individual who can surprise
me with her unique and of-
fensive beauties, not her ex-

sense of humor, Worf's
strength, Riker's height,
Geordi's intelligence and
communicator skills like Picard. I am shapely like Troi.

Robert DeNiro kinda guy.
Seeks woman with Green-
wich Village cool. Little

graduate student, 31. Me:
postmodern hipster, English-
Literature degree, rockabilly,
like waffles. You: must hate
hippies, drunks, frozen yo-
gurt. Cat: black.

Dashing, 31, 6'3", 180lbs,

er former boyfriend!
ails! References availa

50 Meaningful relatio
with cute dyke who ca
air Ford pick-up truck

Unmask, join hands, ju
own, spin around, plur
to the pool? Ecstatic
orpoises? I say we do

WM, 5'10", 200 pou
lack hair eyes. Seekin
mall, all redhead, your
oney. I want the bubb
e coated for us with h
ways.

Those men who cuddle
hores for love are sec
y their darling's charm
only have tired arms f
aying hugged the clo
above.

On the prowl for a mal
not a male line) who's
hite male, 5'7"+, 25-4

WM, 36, seeking pret
oung SWF, sweethear
Need your pollen. My s
ill keep you blooming

Petite white profession
nale, 45, nonsmoking
runette beauty search
or lion king. Scratchin
iting—all possible. Le
or a fili, dance all nig
unt all day.

Rare Violin seeks matc
ow for warm harmonie
encounters. Fretwork in
ludes exceptional qual
reen eyes, auburn hai
trument produces mel
ous, intelligent, witty se
enjoys share shifting

rostbite. Blood type un
ortant. Must like drag
pending some evening
lone.

User-friendly, software
mized for a romantic, l
erm relationship, free

dust off my cover and run her fingers through my pages.

Coach—under 50, conscious, considerate, honest, patient, into snuggling, sailing. Spirited at challenging ladies. Call for tryouts.

that glimmering star to capture me in her gravitational pull. One star planet, will orbit you with affection, his molten core will fuel those passions to keep your sparkle shining. I'm your candidate for...

sense of humor, Worf's strength, Riker's height, Geordi's intelligence and communicator skills like Picard. I am shapely like Troi.

Robert DeNiro kinda guy. Seeks woman with Green-wich Village soul. Little...

resourceful repartees, hip hype. Me,yes, flick star, tune whistlin', natural, flavorful, savvy, funky, tra junkie.

Consider dating me! Every woman I've dated in the last years has ended up with her former boyfriend! Nails! References available...

God, send me an angel, won't tear us apart.

41, colt-less, educated, ssful, attractive, t/weight proportionate, hy.

put on our capes and s and team up for adare! To the Batpoles! rs, Two-Faces and Catian need not apply.

e white male seeks dly Baywatch wannabe knows when to turn it and when to turn it on. ired; mouth to mouth citation.

y 20's woman looking gothic, man who has an ng for the darker things.

le foundation and attive appearance add to uality and charm. Prefy: you are handsome, 33-41, financially, emolly and physically fit, o appreciate!

llector's item, low maintce and some assembly red. Act now, and re- a boomerang demon-ion free! Hurry! Offer ed.

M, 28, tall, slender ngs (brown/blue color ne), Safe for outdoor athletic use. Many ehold uses in garden, shon, kitchen. Travel y (extensively field d overseas).

ear old professional ng for match who's 25- andsome, honest, ma-and not looking for orary source of heat

GWF, 29, avid swimmer ing private investigator, r, is fishing for a an who isn't afraid of eep end.

Hey String Beans. . . . The professor seeks Mary Ann. I was too busy making radios from coconuts to notice you then, but I need you now. Let's gather bamboo and palms and build a life. P.S. I have Howell's ATM number.

50 Meaningful relation ith cute dyke who can a ur Ford pick-up truck.

nmask, join hands, jum own, spin around, plung to the pool? Ecstatic li orpoises? I say we do it

WM, 5'10", 200 poun ack hair, eyes. Seeking tall, all redhead, young oney. I want the bubble coated for us with ho ways.

ose men who cuddle hores for love are seda their darling's charm oily have tired arms fr aving hugged the cloud love.

n the prowl for a male ot a male lined who's s hite male, 5'7"+, 25-4

WM, 56, seeking prett any SWF, sweetheart... eed your pollen. My st ll keep you blooming.

elite white professiona ale, 45, nonsmoking nnette beauty searchi lion king. Scratching ting—all possible. Let r a kill, dance all nigh ut all day.

re Violin seeks matche ow for warm harmonie counters. Fretwork in des exceptional curve en eyes, auburn hair, inment produces melo ue, intelligent, witty so

njoys shape shifting an rostbite. Blood type un portant. Must like drago spending some evening alone.

User-friendly software nized for a romantic, lo term relationship. Prod

1949 or 1953. Better like dogs.

Get your hands dirty with this hot young archaeologist looking for an Indiana Jones to excavate my secret passageways. Must have a mind...

animated cuddlers to hibernate with in the 100 Acre Woods of life.

SM interested in meeting an individual who can surprise me with her unique and offensive beauties, not her ex...

graduate student, 31. Me: postmodern hipster, English-Literature degree, rockabilly, like waffles. You: must hate hippies, drunks, frozen yogurt. Cat: black.

Dashing, 31, 6'3", 180lbs,

TV SCI-FI LOVE

Dashing Starfleet Captain— SBM, 36, seeks passionate, full-figured lady for first officer. Any race/species. 25–40. For serious love among the stars. Pointed ears optional. Engage and make it so.

Beam Me Up Scotty!

There's no suitable life down here! I've looked all over for a woman that is adventurous, outgoing, petite, enjoys dining out, movies, Rollerblading, and sci-fi. Please respond or I'll destroy your planet! (Species unimportant.)

God, send me an angel, won't tear us apart.

41, colt-less, educated, essful, attractive, ht/weight proportionate, thy.

s put on our capes and s and team up for ad- ure! To the Batpoles! rs, Two-Faces and Cat- an need not apply.

le white male seeks dly Baywatch wannabe knows when to turn it nd when to turn it on. ired; mouth to mouth scitation.

y 20's woman looking gothic man who has an ng for the darker things.

le foundation and at- ive appearance add to uality and charm. Pre- fy: you are handsome, 33-41, financially, emo- ally and physically fit, o appreciate!

llector's item, low main- nce and some assembly ired. Act now, and re- e a boomerang demon- ion free! Hurry! Offer ed.

er, 28, tall, slender ngs (brown/blue color nie). Safe for outdoor athletic use. Many ehold uses in garden, shop, kitchen. Travel y (extensively field ed overseas).

ear oldprofessional ling for match who's 25- andsome, honest, ma- and not looking for orary source of heat

GWF, 29, avid swimmer ling private investigator, looking for a an who isn't afraid of leep end.

dust off my cover and run her fingers through my pages.

Coach–under 50, conscious, considerate, honest, patient, into snuggling, sailing. Spir- ited at challenging ladies. Call for tryouts.

that glimmering star to cap- ture me in her gravitational pull. One star planet, will orbit you with affection, his molten core will fuel those passions to keep your sparkle shining.

I'm your candidate for...

1949 or 1953. Better like dogs.

Get your hands dirty with this hot young archaeologist looking for an Indiana Jones to excavate my secret pas- sageways. Must have a mind

more than now seeks other animated cuddlers to hiber- nate with in the 100 Acre Woods of life.

SM interested in meeting an individual who can surprise me with her unique and of- fensive beauties, not her ex-

sense of humor, Worf's strength, Riker's height, Geordi's intelligence and communicator skills like Pi- card. I am shapely like Troi.

Robert DeNiro kinda guy. Seeks woman with Green- wich Village soul. I like

graduate student, 31. Me: postmodern hipster, English- Literature degree, rockabilly, like waffles. You: must hate hippies, drunks, frozen yo- gurt. Cat: black.

Dashing, 31, 6'3", 180lbs,

resourceful repartees, not hype. Me, yes, flick sin th', tune whistlin', natur flavorful, savvy, funky, tr junkie.

Consider dating me! Ev woman I've dated in the e years has ended up r former boyfriend! N ls! References availab

0 Meaningful relation th cute dyke who can ir Ford pick-up truck.

nmask, join hands, jun wn, spin around, plun o the pool? Ecstatic rpoises? I say we do i

WA, 5'10", 200 poun ick hair, eyes. Seeking ail, all redhead, youn ney. I want the hubbie coated for us with ho ways.

ose men who cuddle ores for love are seda their darling's charm nly have tired arms f ving hugged the cloud ove.

the prowl for a male of a male line) who's s ite male, 5'7"+, 25-4

WM, 36, seeking prett ing SWF, sweetheart eed your pollen. My st ll keep you blooming.

tite white professiona ale, 45, nonsmoking nnette beauty searchi r lion King. Scratching ling – all possible. Le r a kill, dance all nigh nt all day.

re Violin seeks match w for warm harmonie counters. Fretwork in udes exceptional curv een eyes, auburn hair. ument produces mele s, intelligent, witty so

njoys shape shifting an ostbite. Blood type ur portant. Must like drag spending some evening a one.

User-friendly, software mized for a romantic, lo term relationship. Proc

The Borgs are Here!!!!

GWM 27 seeks compatible entity to offer protection against the threat of assimilation. If you are seeking new life, I will boldly take you where no one has gone before.

Captain Picard Looking for Vash. Mid-twenties, Starfleet Captain, well-traveled, highly educated, versed on a number of subjects, with a very loose interpretation of the Prime Directive. Seeking charming, intelligent, articulate, clever, fun rogue to share time on holodecks and raisha.

God, send me an angel, won't tear us apart.

41, colt-less, educated, cessful, attractive, nt/weight proportionate, thy.

s put on our capes and s and team up for ad- ure! To the Batpoles! rs, Two-Faces and Cat- an need not apply.

le white male seeks dly Baywatch wannabe knows when to turn it nd when to turn it on. uired: mouth to mouth scitation.

y 20's woman looking gothic man who has an ng for the darker things

le foundation and at- tive appearance add to uality and charm. Pre- ify: you are handsome, 33-41, financially, emo- ally and physically fit, o appreciate!

llector's item, low main- nce and some assembly ired. Act now, and re- e a boomerang demon- tion free! Hurry! Offer ed.

M, 28, tall, slender ngs (brown/blue color me). Safe for outdoor athletic use. Many ehold uses in garden, kshop, kitchen. Travel y (extensively field d overseas).

ear oldprofessional ing for match who's 25- andsome, honest, ma- and not looking for orary source of heat

GWF, 29, avid swimmer ling private investigator, er, is fishing for a an who isn't afraid of deep end.

dust on my cover and run her fingers through my pages.

Coach—under 50, conscious, considerate, honest, patient, into snuggling, sailing. Spir- ited at challenging ladies.

that glimmering star to cap- ture me in her gravitational pull. One star planet, will orbit you with affection, his molten core will fuel those passions to keep your sparkle shining.

1949 or 1953. Better like dogs.

Get your hands dirty with this hot young archaeologist looking for an Indiana Jones to excavate my secret pas- sageways. Must have a mind

more than her. Seeks some animated cuddlers to hiber- nate with in the 100 Acre Woods of life.

SM interested in meeting an individual who can surprise me with her unique and of- fensive beauties, not her ex-

sense of humor, Wort's strength, Riker's height, Geordi's intelligence and communicator skills like Pi- card. I am shapely like Troi.

Robert DeNiro kinda guy. Seeks woman with Green- wich Village cool. Little

graduate student, 31. Me: postmodern hipster; English- Literature degree, rockabilly, like waffles. You: must hate hippies, drunks, frozen yo- gurt. Cat: black.

Dashing, 31, 6'3", 180lbs,

resourceful repartees, no hype. Me, yes, flick si tin', tune whistlin', natur flavorful, savvy, funky, tr junkie.

Consider dating me! Eve woman I've dated in the e years has ended up former boyfriend! N ils! References availab

0 Meaningful relatio th cute dyke who can ir Ford pick-up truck.

mask, join hands, jur wn, spin around, plun o the pool? Ecstatic rpoises? I say we do i

WM, 5'10", 200 poun ack hair, eyes. Seeking all, all redhead, youn ney, I want the bubble coated for us with ho ways.

ose men who cuddle ores for love are seda their darling's charm nly have tired arms f aving hugged the clou ove.

n the prowl for a male ot a male line) who's s ite male, 5'7"+, 25-4

WM, 36, seeking prett ung SWF, sweetheart eed your pollen. My s ll keep you blooming.

tite white profession ale, 45, nonsmoking unette beauty searchi lion king. Scratchin ting—all possible. Le a hill, dance all nigh nt all day.

re Violin seeks matc w for warm harmonic counters. Fretwork ir des exceptional curv een eyes, auburn hair rument produces mele s, intelligent, witty so

njoys shape shifting a rostbite. Blood type u portant. Must like drag pending some evening alone.

User-friendly, software mized for a romantic, l term relationship. Proc

Boldly Go Marriage . . .
. . . the final frontier. To seek out new adventures and boldly go where no woman has gone before. This is the voyage of the seeking single. No cling-ons—warp speed. Call me!

X-Phile—Statuesque Scully seeks Mulder to continue the search on the dark side of Dallas. Looking for aliens, vampires, evil twins, and metal nose implants. Staying away from geeks and humanoid leeches. The truth is out there. So am I!

Alien Abduction—Fox Mulder type seeks X-File. The truth is out there, so is a sexy 25–35-year-old alien. Me, 30-year-old agent, 6′, WM, into world travel and NW. Shorter, dark-haired aliens preferred, cancer man need not.

dust off my cover and run her fingers through my pages.
Coach—under 50, conscious, considerate, honest, patient, into snuggling, sailing. Spirited at challenging ladies.

that glimmering star to capture in her gravitational pull. One star planet, will orbit you with affection, his molten core will fuel those passions to keep your sparkle shining.

sense of humor, Worf's strength, Riker's height, Geordi's intelligence and communicator skills like Picard. I am shapely like Troi.
Robert DeNiro kinda guy. Seeks woman with Green-

resourceful repartees, not hype. Me,yes, flick s tin', tune whistlin', natu flavorful, savvy, funky, th junkie.
Consider dating me! Ev woman I've dated in th e years has ended up r former boyfriend! M ils! References availa

WATCH TV WITH ME

No repeats—SWJF, 27.

M: Melrose; McBeal

T: NewsRadio

W: 90210/Party of Five

Th: Must See TV

F/S: Buckhead, Highlands

Su: Simpsons or movie.

1949 or 1953. Better like dogs.

more than just a other animated cuddlers to hibernate with in the 100 Acre Woods of life.

graduate student, 31. Me: postmodern hipster, English Literature degree, rockabilly, like waffles. You: must hate hippies, drinks, frozen yogurt. Cat: black.

I'm a cool guy, and spend lots of time watching network TV. Most of the women I love are TV stars. Some are models. If you're looking for a guy who is like that doctor dude of that hospital show, ya know, the one that was in that crappy movie with Michelle Pfeiffer (I love her!), a guy who works with computers and smokes and drinks a lot, and if you don't really like guys who exercise but are still thin, and if you like guys that don't have much money, then call me, but only if you're hot. Oh yeah, I'm not greedy.

NewsHour—Attractive, 36, PF, with life, seeks acquaintance with gentleman, 38–48. Must watch the NewsHour with Jim Lehrer regularly and at times, in response to a particularly insightful report on genocide or the proliferation of chemical weapons, has risen from his chair and immediately, almost involuntarily, mailed a check to public television. Male pattern balding not a problem; preferable actually.

p with one bright,
easy to look at, easy
with SWM feathered
(43-55).

dust off my cover and run
her fingers through my
pages.

Coach—under 50, conscious,
considerate, honest, patient,
into snuggling, sailing. Spirited at challenging ladies.

that glimmering star to capture me in her gravitational
pull. One star planet, will
orbit you with affection, his
molten core will fuel those
passions to keep your
sparkle shining.

I'm your candidate for

sense of humor, Worf's
strength, Riker's height,
Geordi's intelligence and
communicator skills like Picard. I am shapely like Troi.

Robert DeNiro kinda guy.
Seeks woman with Green-

Television Addict—Single white male seeks friendly Baywatch wannabe who knows when to turn it off and when to turn it on. Required: mouth-to-mouth resuscitation. Optional: swimming, crime fighting, and artificial enhancements.

lood—This charming
7 seeks the perfect
d new lover with lips
gar, "boy meets girl"
od, send me an ange
on't tear us apart.

, colt-less, educated,
sful, attractive,
weight proportionat
y.

but on our capes and
and team up for ad-
e! To the Batpoles!
, Two-Faces and Cat-
i need not apply.

white male seeks
y Baywatch wannabe
ows when to turn it
d when to turn it on.
ed: mouth to mouth
tation.

20's woman looking
othic man who has a
for the darker thing

foundation and at-
appearance add to
ality and charm. Pre-
: you are handsome,
3-41, financially, emo
y and physically fit,
appreciate!

ector's item, low mai
e and some assembl
ed. Act now, and re-
boomerang demon-
n free! Hurry! Offer

28, tall, slender
s (brown/blue color
). Safe for outdoor
hletic use. Many
old uses in garden,
op, kitchen. Travel
extensively field
overseas).

r oldprofessional
g for match who's 25
idsome, honest, ma-
not looking for
ary source of heat

1949 or 1953. Better like
dogs.

Get your hands dirty with
this hot young archaeologist
looking for an Indiana Jones
to excavate my secret pas-
sageways. Must have a mind

animated cuddlers to hiber-
nate with in the 100 Acre
Woods of life.

SM interested in meeting an
individual who can surprise
me with her unique and of-
fensive beauties, not her

graduate student, 31. Me:
postmodern hipster, English-
Literature degree, rockabilly,
like waffles. You: must hate
hippies, drunks, frozen yo-
gurt. Cat: black.

Dashing, 31, 6'3", 180lbs.

r former boyfriend! Ne
ails! References availab

50 Meaningful relationsh
with cute dyke who can r
pair Ford pick-up truck.

Unmask, join hands, jum
down, spin around, plunge
into the pool? Ecstatic li
porpoises? I say we do it

SWM, 5'10", 200 pound
black hair, eyes. Seeking
small, all redhead, young
honey. I want the bubble
e coated for us with hon
always.

Those men who cuddle
whores for love are sedat
y their darling's charms
only have tired arms fr
having hugged the clouds
above.

On the prowl for a male li
not a male line) who's sl
white male, 5'7"+, 25-40

SWM, 36, seeking pretty
young SWF, sweetheart.
Need your pollen. My sti
will keep you blooming.

Petite white professional
male, 45, nonsmoking
brunette beauty searchin
or lion king. Scratching
biting—all possible. Let's
or a kill, dance all night,
unt all day.

Rare Violin seeks matchi
bow for warm harmonio
encounters. Fretwork in-
cludes exceptional curve
green eyes, auburn hair. I
strument produces melod
ous, intelligent, witty sou

rostbite. Blood type unir
portant. Must like dragon
pending some evening
alone.

User-friendly, software d
nized for a romantic, lon
erm relationship. Proce

WF, 29, avid swimme
private investigato
is fishing for a
ho isn't afraid of
p end.

LOVE BITES

Another very popular themed ad.
There are so many vampires out there looking for love, now I'm scared to go out at night.
(Bold emphasis added.)

Slacker **Vampire** Type seeks woman for nocturnal meanderings, feeding frenzies, and general lascivious behavior in public. Not gothic and not desperate. Just looking for fun. Must show well.

Kiss Me, Kiss Me, Kiss Me—Early 20's woman looking for a gothic man who has an inkling for the darker things. Blood red lips, pale skin, black velvet, soft sheets. Looking for my **vampire** love to take me to a passionate place where I have never been.

Vampiric, Dark Knight, gothic SWM, 6 ft. 3 in., slender, brown hair w/eyes of the stars. Adventurous as James Bond, words of Jim Morrison, and romantic as **Dracula**. Seeking midnight princess to share the night together, share their feelings, their dreams. Respond and I will whisper you poems under the moonlight.

Lady **Vampire**—Tall, pale, long blonde, blue, 25 SWF ISO tall, thin, 25–28 SWM, Alice Cooper look-alike. Only long-haired men need apply.

Transylvanian Concubine wanted by SWM long dark-haired, tall, sensual artist, 30's into Rasputina, sex, Dead Can Dance, Nature, sex, candles, **vampires**, ethnic foods, Sisters of Mercy, and red wine for eternal bliss. Any race, healthy NS only.

Graveyard Scenes—SWF, seeks androgynous, Bowiesque **vampire** for graveyard scenes. Be beautiful, articulate, gentleman of substance. I'm a petite woman on a spiritual pilgrimage. Call me and get an interview with this Gothic Blonde. Hot.

Undead European male with lovely pair of dogteeth, pine-matted blond mane and much, much less seeks winter princess of Wallachia. Enjoys shape shifting and frostbite. Blood type unimportant. Must like dragons, spending some evenings alone.

HOUSE OF LOVE

Handyman's Special—Cute as a button, this 30+ yr. old dwelling just became available. Solid foundation exudes quality and old-world interior appeal. Vacant for some time, now ready to be lived in. Needs light repairs and TLC, bring all the right tools. Owner selective but open to all bids. Call, come see!

On The Market—Well kept property, 33 by 5′x 6″, brown roof and green shutters, won't last long. Stable foundation and attractive appearance add to the quality and charm. Pre-qualify: you are handsome, 6′+, 33–41, financially, emotionally, and physically fit, see to appreciate!

New Home on Market—
This gorgeous 29 year old home features olive skin tone paint, hazel lights, dark wavy black carpet, and humorous doorbell. If you are attractive single female, 24–33, who is witty and fun, contact the realtor today for more information.

Investment Property— Horse property, wide open views, rustic ranch, glowing fireplaces, good strong foundation, large family room, shows clean, circa 1957, solid plumbing, strong electric connections, full modern library, good-clean-working appliances.

Old Fixer-Upper. Not me, my house. Bought one with great potential, but the remodeling I'm planning could really use a woman's touch (as could I). Myself? I'm a creative professional SWM . . . 39 . . . dark hair on the roof, baby blue windows (eyes), proportionate to my lot size with lots of interesting nooks and crannies. I feature a solid foundation (but plenty of parking for new ideas), nice warm furnace, excellent view on life, no mortgaged future and I'm in move-in condition. Won't last. Call now.

For lease: 1966 Single, 6′ 2″ ceilings, blond/blue decor, charming and attractive atmosphere, perfect for SWF, 25–30, month-to-month lease with option to buy.

Serious Buyers Only—Majestic contemporary, GWM, 1955 quality construction, maintained to perfection, seeking newer ranch model, built 1960–1970, A-1 condition, fabulous. Appts. for private showing now being taken.

Desirable property—with character! Needs attention, 1965 model, color—white with blond/blue trim, tall, with very little wear and tear. Seeking SWF under 30 and thin for LTR. Interested?

BUY ME!

Attention O-Mart Shoppers—This unique, pink light special, produced mid-1940's, is attractively packaged in white, blue, and gold, quality controlled, fire-retardant and amazingly portable! A collector's item, low maintenance and some assembly required. Act now, and receive a boomerang demonstration free! Hurry! Offer limited.

Available Now! One nice guy, 28. New merchandise, not used! Limited time offered. Last one in stock. Don't let this offer pass you by! Call before it's too late.

ship with one bright,
y, easy to look at, easy
e with SWM feathered
nd (43-55).

blood– This charming
37 seeks the perfect F
and new lover with lips
sugar, "boy meets girl"
Gold, send me an angel
won't tear us apart.

41, coit-less, educated,
cessful, attractive,
ht/weight proportionate
thy.

s put on our capes and
is and team up for ad-
ure! To the Batpoles!
ers, Two-Faces and Cat-
nan need not apply.

gle white male seeks
ndly Baywatch wannabe
knows when to turn it
and when to turn it on.
uired: mouth to mouth
scitation.

ly 20's woman looking
a gothic man who has a
ing for the darker thing

ple foundation and at-
tive appearance add to
quality and charm. Pre-
ify: you are handsome,
, 33-41, financially, emo
ally and physically fit,
to appreciate!

ollector's item, low mai
ance and some assembl
uired. Act now, and re-
e a boomerang demon-
tion free! Hurry! Offer
ted.

M, 28, tall, slender
ngs (brown/blue color
me). Safe for outdoor
athletic use. Many
ehold uses in garden,
kshop, kitchen. Travel
ly (extensively field
ed overseas).

year oldprofessional
king for match who's 25
handsome, honest, ma-
and not looking for
porary source of heat

GWF, 29, avid swimmer
ding private investigato
er, is fishing for a
nan who isn't afraid of
deep end.

dust off my cover and run
her fingers through my
pages.

Coach–under 50, conscious,
considerate, honest, patient,
into snuggling, sailing. Spirited at challenging ladies.
Call for tryouts.

1949 or 1953. Better like
dogs.

Get your hands dirty with
this hot young archaeologist
looking for an Indiana Jones
to excavate my secret pas-
sageways. Must have a mind

that glimmering star to capture me in her gravitational
pull. One star planet, will
orbit you with affection, his
molten core will fuel those
passions to keep your
sparkle shining.

I'm your candidate for

animated cuddlers to hiber-
nate with in the 100 Acre
Woods of life.

SM interested in meeting an
individual who can surprise
me with her unique and of-
fensive beauties, not her ex-

sense of humor, Worf's
strength, Riker's height,
Geordi's intelligence and
communicator skills like Picard. I am shapely like Troi.

Robert DeNiro kinda guy.
Seeks woman with Green-
wich Village cool. Little

graduate student, 31. Me:
postmodern hipster, English-
Literature degree, rockabilly,
like waffles. You: must hate
hippies, drunks, frozen yo-
gurt. Cat: black.

Dashing, 31, 6'3", 180lbs,

Unlimited Warranty—
This adventurous, attractive,
easy-going DWM, 36, is
warranted to be free from
defects under normal use
for a period not to exceed
one lifetime. Warranty void
if subjected to misuse or
neglect. Warranty applies
only to S/DWF.

her former boyfriend!
ails! References avail

50 Meaningful relatio
with cute dyke who ca
air Ford pick-up truc

Unmask, join hands, ju
down, spin around, plu
nto the pool? Ecstatic
orpoises? I say we do

WM, 5'10", 200 pou
lack hair, eyes. Seekir
mall, all redhead, you
oney. I want the bubb
e coated for us with t
always.

hose men who cuddl
whores for love are see
their darling's char
only have tired arms
aving hugged the clo
bove.

n the prowl for a mal
not a male line) who's
white male, 5'7" +, 25-

WM, 36, seeking
oung SWF, sweethear
Need your patien. My
ill keep you blooming

Petite white professio
male, 45, nonsmoking
runette beauty search
or lion king. Scratchi
iting—all possible. L
or a kill, dance all nig
unt all day.

Rare Violin seeks
ow for warm harmon
encounters. Fretwork
ludes exceptional cu
reen eyes, auburn hai
trument produces me
us, intelligent, witty s
njoys share shifting

ostbite. Blood type i
ortant. Must like dr
pending some evening
lone.

User-friendly, softwa
nized for a romantic,
rm relationship. Pro

Not sold in stores! SWM, 28, tall, slender stylings (brown/blue color scheme). Safe for outdoor and athletic use. Many household uses in garden, workshop, kitchen. Travel ready (extensively field tested overseas). Caution: tears through books. Perfect for SWF, 25+, who has (almost) everything. Call now! Operators are standing by!

Attention Shoppers, On Aisle 27 about 5′ 5″ off the floor, we have this special item that every male should ask for. It weighs about 110 lbs. You can take it to the movies, sporting events, dancing, etc. This item can be bought by any race, satisfaction guaranteed.

Preseason Special—Prepare for fall. Warm, cuddly 30ish single guy now available. Features include multi-ethnic styling, easy programmability, low maintenance requirements, excellent communication skills, and more. Offer valid for all single women. Supply is limited, so call now!

New from Ronco!

It slices, dices, and satisfies. Well built and rust proof! It's the Automatic Lover! Just in time for X-mas! No batteries needed! Going fast! Call now!

Male Order—Order yours in time for the holidays. For those shopping for that special someone. This product tested for over 40 years with only one complaint. Handsome design, comes in salt and pepper only. Test market. Attractive, slender female seeking product reliability, not liability. Satisfaction guaranteed. Offer expires soon.

Imperatives

Some ads make specific demands like "you must . . ." or other imperatives. While most are obvious and reasonable—"must like dogs" or "nonsmokers only"—others, like those listed here, are a little odder.

Relationship Demands

[Must be] willing to let me have the last word when I need it

Must be neat, positive, understandable

You must possess the qualities of Jesus and Sting combined

Must desire a 360 degree relationship

Inward grace a must

Out of control passion a must!

Needs someone who respects death

Must have better morals than Clinton's

Work Demands

Must be unafraid of power tools

Big bonus if you are involved in or have an interest in real estate foreclosure

Must work on a railroad

State troopers only

Must have desire to work on motorbikers' rights

Strong shoulders helpful

Shotgun useful; gun safety mandatory

Library retrieval literate, please

Arts and Letters Demands

[Must] appreciate Jack London's soul, depth, sensitivity, and heart

Must play ukulele or be willing to learn

Must have knowledge of Chevy Chase films

Stephen King freak a must

Must have dance video shape

You must like Bingo

You must respect Marilyn Manson

Looks Demands

Must have big "backyard"

[Must] have perpetual flat stomach

Hairy legs a must

Must have hair/teeth; implants ok

Must love nudity at home (sometimes) but especially in wooded areas of Northern California

Only those with Klingon honor, passion, looks need apply

Must have mind, body, and spirit

Must have shoulder-length Breck hair

Miscellaneous Demands:

Must know what a bubbler is

Isn't afraid to look fear in the face

Must have truck

Must be willing to give the President a second chance

Must enjoy drinking malt liquor

Must like feet

PC-ness required

Must be able to pass crucial best friend's husband test

Must pass the test of fire with my three big dogs

Chronic pain a plus!

Must know meaning of LIFE!

Please drive a sport utility vehicle

Perfect childhoods are rare—otherwise, please be or have been in therapy

LOVE CRIMES

Unusual Suspect—Convicted romantic on probation. Tall, attractive, athletic, sensuous PWSM, 45, seeks similar SWF probation officer 25–40, for mutual rehabilitation program. Court ordered activities to include spontaneous outings, baths for two, abundant laughter, etc. Life sentence possible.

Arrest Me Officer—Police ISO suspect. The suspect is good-looking, GW/HM, 26–40, straight acting, in shape, romantic, honest, caring, relationship-minded, fun and dedicated. The cop: 37, 5′ 9″/160, blonde/green, athletic into sports, travel, and fun. If you fit the profile, turn yourself in. Please call.

Pyromaniac seeks extra spark to kindle wintertime fires together, possibly more. 30 year old professional looking for match who's 25–30, handsome, honest, mature, and not looking for temporary source of heat. Real firemen only—no flamers.

Casanova Indicted on love crimes charge. Legendary romantic, sensual kisser, UNT grad, 26, 5′ 9″, 225 lbs., brown hair, brown eyes pleads guilty. Handsome, honest lover seeks daring, intelligent, attractive partner, 23–40, for romantic getaways and pleasurable offenses. Repeat offenders encouraged.

Partner in Crime to hold up 9:30 Club, Capital Ballroom, theaters, festivals, small dives, live events, HFS. Steal views from museums, parks, and other natural treasures. Getaway via bike, country drive, sailing (the fall is always great), skiing, run. Attractive SWM, 33 y.o., 5 ft. 9 in., medium build, blue eyes. No experience necessary.

ur God, send me an angel.
e won't tear us apart.

1 41, colt-less, educated,
ccessful, attractive,
ght/weight proportionate,
althy.

t's put on our capes and
wls and team up for ad-
nture! To the Batpoles!
kers, Two-Faces and Cat-
man need not apply.

ngle white male seeks
endly Baywatch wannabe
o knows when to turn it
i and when to turn it on,
quired, mouth to mouth
uscitation.

rly 20's woman fool ing
r a gothic man who has a
cling for the darker things

able foundation and at-
active appearance add to
r quality and charm. Pre-
ally: you are handsome,
., 33-41, financially, emo-
nally and physically fit,
e to appreciate!

collector's item, low main
ance and some assembly
quired. Act now, and re-
ve a boomerang demon-
ation free! Hurry! Offer
ited.

VM, 28, tall, slender
lings brown/blue-color
nemel. Safe for outdoor
d athletic use. Many
usehold uses in garden,
rkshop, kitchen. Travel
ady (extensively held
sted overseas).

year old professional
oking for match who's 25-
, handsome, honest, ma-
re and not looking for
nporary source of heat

is GWF, 29, avid swimmer
dding private investigator,
cer, is fishing for a
oman who isn't afraid of
e deep end.

dust off my cover and run
her fingers through my
pages.

Coach—under 50, conscious,
considerate, honest, patient,
into snuggling, sailing. Spirited at challenging ladies.
Call for tennis.

that glimmering star to capture me in her gravitational
pull. One star planet, will
orbit your with affection, his
molten core will fuel those
passions to keep your
sparkle shining.

I'm your candidate for...

1949 or 1953. Better like
dogs.

Get your hands dirty with
this hot young archaeologist
looking for an Indiana Jones
to excavate my secret pas-
sageways. Must have a mind

animated cuddlers to hiber-
nate with in the 100 Acre
Woods of life.

SM interested in meeting an
individual who can surprise
me with her unique and of-
fensive beauties, not her ex-

sense of humor, Worf's
strength, Riker's height,
Geordi's intelligence and
communicator skills like Picard. I am shapely like Troi.

Robert DeNiro kinda guy.
Seeks woman with Green-
wich Village cool. Little

graduate student, 31. Me:
postmodern hipster, English-
Literature degree, rockabilly,
like waffles. You: must hate
hippies, drunks, frozen yo-
gurt. Cat: black.

Dashing, 31, 6'3", 180lbs,

resourceful repartees,
not hype. Me, yes, flick
in', tune whistlin', nat
flavorful, savvy, funky
junkie.

Consider dating me! E
woman I've dated in th
ve years has ended u
r former boyfriend!
ils! References avail

50 Meaningful relati
th cute dyke who ca
ir Ford pick-up truc

nmask, join hands, ju
own, spin around, plu
to the pool? Ecstati
urposes? I say we do

WM, 5'10", 200 pou
ack hair, eyes. Seekin
mall, all redhead, you
oney. I want the bubb
coated for us with r
ways.

ose men who cuddl
hores for love are se
y their darling's char
only have tired arms
aving hugged the clo
ove.

n the prowl for a ma
ct a male line? who'
hite male, 5'7", 25

WM, 36, seeking pre
ung SWF, sweethea
eed your pollen. My
ll keep you bloomin

etite white professio
ole, 45, nonsmo inc
unette beauty searc
r lion king. Scratch
ting—all possible, L
r a kill, dance all ni
unt all day.

are Violin seeks mae
ow for warm harmo
counters. Fretwork
ludes exceptional c
een eyes, auburn ha
rument produces me
s, Intelligent, witty

njoys shape shifting
ostblite. Blood type
portant. Must like de
sending some evenin
one.

ser-friendly, softwa
rized for a romantic
rm relationship. Pro

Wanted Man—Crime: Celibacy. Description: athlete, 6′ 1″, 180 lbs., 34, blonde, green eyes, visits museums, comedy clubs, beaches. ISO: athletic SWF in crime.

Most Wanted! Professional SWM, 29, 6′, 165, disarming personality, attractive, ready to surrender to athletic, clever, spontaneous, intelligent, fun-loving SWF for possible life sentence.

Are you tall, dark, handsome and own your own handcuffs? Cute professional, full-figured SWF, 24, seeks single, burly police officer or sheriff, sense of humor, positive attitude a must. No rent-a-cops please.

dust off my cover and run her fingers through my pages.

Coach—under 50, conscious, considerate, honest, patient, into snuggling, sailing. Spirited at challenging ladies. Call for layouts.

that glimmering star to capture me in her gravitational pull. One star planet, will orbit you with affection, his molten core will fuel those passions to keep your sparkle shining.

I'm your candidate for

sense of humor, Worf's strength, Riker's height, Geordi's intelligence and communicator skills like Picard. I am shapely like Troi.

Robert DeNiro kinda guy. Seeks woman with Greenwich Village cool. Little

resourceful repartees, not hype. Me,yes, flick tin', tune whistlin', nat flavorful, savvy, funky, junkie.

Consider dating me! E woman I've dated in t ve years has ended u er former boyfriend! als! References avail

ar God, send me an angel, e won't tear us apart.

41, colt-less, educated, ccessful, attractive, ght/weight proportionate, althy.

's put on our capes and wls and team up for ad nture! To the Batpoles! eers, Two-Faces and Catman need not apply.

ngle white male seeks endly Baywatch wannabe o knows when to turn it and when to turn it on quired; mouth to mouth uscitation.

rly 20's woman looking a gothic man who has an ding for the darker things

able foundation and at-ctive appearance add to quality and charm. Pre-ality; you are handsome, , 33-41, financially, emo-nally and physically fit, e to appreciate!

collector's item, low main ance and some assembly quired. Act now, and re-ve a boomerang demon-ration free! Hurry! Offer ited.

VM, 28, tall, slender rlings (brown/blue color ieme). Safe for outdoor d athletic use. Many usehold uses in garden, rkshop, kitchen. Travel ady (extensively field sted overseas).

year oldprofessional oking for match who's 25-, handsome, honest, ma-re and not looking for mporary source of heat

is GWF, 29, avid swimmer rlings (brown/blue color ncer, is fishing for a man who isn't afraid of deep end.

50 Meaningful relati th cute dyke who ca air Ford pick-up truc

nmask, join hands, ju own, spin around, plu to the pool? Ecstatic orpoises? I say we de

WM, 5'10", 200 pos ack hair, eyes. Seek all, all redhead, yo ney, I want the bul coaled for us with ways.

hose men who cuddl hores for love are se their darling's char only have tired arms ving hugged the clo ove.

n the prowl for a ma ot a male line) who' hite male, 5'7"+, 25

WM, 36, seeking pre oung SWF, sweethea eed your pollen. My Il keep you bloomin

etite white professic le, 45, nonsmoking unette beauty searc r lion Fling. Scratch ting—all possible. L r a kill, dance all ni int all day.

re Violin seeks mat ow for warm harmo counters. Fretwork des exceptional cu een eyes, auburn h rument produces m s, intelligent, witty

ijoys shape shifting ostbite. Blood type portant. Must like dr spending some eveni one.

1949 or 1953. Better like dogs.

Get your hands dirty with this hot young archaeologist looking for an Indiana Jones to excavate my secret pas-sageways. Must have a mind

animated cuddlers to hiber-nate with in the 100 Acre Woods of life.

SM interested in meeting an individual who can surprise me with her unique and of-fensive beauties, not her ex-

graduate student, 31. Me: postmodern hipster, English-Literature degree, rockabilly, like waffles. You: must hate hippies, drunks, frozen yo-gurt. Cat: black.

Dashing, 31, 6'3", 180lbs.

User-friendly, softwa nized for a romantic rm relationship. Pre

Wanted Alive: Dream Woman—Armed and dangerously attractive, early 20s. Suspect is athletic and has a penchant for fun. She's very difficult to identify since many of her qualities are subtle and sly. Notify me immediately for positive identification.

Arresting Personality—Tall, curvaceous brunette seeks non-smoking Caucasian or Hispanic male, 5′ 10″+, 35–45 for possible undercover operation. Great legs for fast pursuits, big brown eyes, and high IQ for finding evidence. This young F, divorced professional is ready for in-depth investigation and high speed chases. Let's interrogate.

AQUA-LOVE

Mermaid Seeks Same—for aquatic adventures. Tired of Wash. DC dating pool. This GWF, 29, avid swimmer, budding private investigator, fencer, is fishing for a woman who isn't afraid of the deep end. Chickens of the sea need not apply.

Water You Doing?—
SWF, 28, with splashy personality & aquatic interests is waving at you! Enjoys being tide up or castled, looking for no drips, 25–35, n/s, to pour my tsunami of love upon. Darling, you sand me!

Near Tide—Find me in the littoral zone, washed up among the bladderwrack. Show me to your hydric home, halospheric sea shack. And when the sun has bleached all bones, night will steal the beach back. I'll leave you wrapped in seaweed sheets, alone, to swim to sleep.

Passionfish seeks angelfish, goldfish, or even reformed piranha for company on the swim upstream. I'm 38, WM, handsome, unencumbered. Enjoy biking, ocean, alternative music.

Catch of the Day—
This 39-year old Doll-fin is looking for his mermaid to travel (I work for an airline), see movies, hold hands, and exercise with. I am not a crab or a whale so drop me a line. Today!

ip with one bright, easy to look at, easy with SWM feathered (43-55).

blood–This charming 37 seeks the perfect F and new lover with lips ugar; "boy meets girl" God, send me an angel von't tear us apart.

1, colt-less, educated, ssful, attractive, t/weight proportionate ly.

put on our capes and and team up for ad-el To the Batpoles! s, Two-Faces and Cat-n need not apply.

white male seeks ly Baywatch wannabe nows when to turn it d when to turn it on. red; mouth to mouth itation.

20's woman looking gothic man who has a g for the darker thing

foundation and at-e appearance add to ality and charm. Pre z: you are handsome, 3-41, financially, emo ly and physically fit, appreciate!

ector's item, low mai ce and some assembly ed. Act now, and re-a boomerang demon-n tree! Hurry! Offer d.

28, tall, slender s (brown/blue color e). Safe for outdoor hletic use. Many hold uses in garden, hop, kitchen. Travel (extensively field overseas).

ar oldprofessional g for match who's 25 ndsome, honest, ma-nd not looking for rary source of heat.

WF, 29, avid swimmer g private investigato is fishing for a o who isn't afraid of ep end.

dust off my cover and run her fingers through my pages.

Coach–under 50, conscious, considerate, honest, patient, into snuggling, sailing. Spir-ited at challenging ladies. Call for tryouts.

1949 or 1953. Better like dogs.

Get your hands dirty with this hot young archaeologist looking for an Indiana Jones to excavate my secret pas-sageways. Must have a mind

that glimmering star to cap-ture me in her gravitational pull. One star planet, will orbit you with affection, his molten core will fuel those passions to keep your sparkle shining.

I'u your candidate for

animated cuddlers to hiber-nate with in the 100 Acre Woods of life.

SM interested in meeting an individual who can surprise me with her unique and of-fensive beauties, not her

sense of humor, Worf's strength, Riker's height, Geordi's intelligence and communicator skills like Pi-card. I am shapely like Troi. Robert DeNiro kinda guy. Seeks woman with Green-wich Village cool. Little

graduate student, 31. Me: postmodern hipster, English-Literature degree, rockabilly, like waffles. You: must hate hippies, drunks, frozen yo-gurt. Cat: black.

Dashing 31, 6'3", 190lbs

er former boyfriend! No ils! References availab

50 Meaningful relations with cute dyke who can r air Ford pick-up truck

unmask, join hands, jum own, spin around, plung nto the pool? Ecstatic orpoises? I say we do it

SWM, 5'10", 200 poun lack hair, eyes. Seeking mall, all redhead, young oney. I want the bubble e coated for us with hor lways.

Those men who cuddle hores for love are sedat y their darling's charms only have tired arms fr aving hugged the clouds bove.

n the prowl for a male li not a male line) who's si hite male, 5'7"+, 25-40

SWM, 36, seeking pretty oung SWF, sweetheart. Need your pollen. My sti will keep you blooming.

Petite white professional male, 45, nonsmoking brunette beauty searching or lion king. Scratching tting—all possible. Let's or a kill, dance all night. unt all day.

Rare Violin seeks matchi ow for warm harmoniou ncounters. Fretwork in-ludes exceptional curves reen eyes, auburn hair. I trument produces melod us, intelligent, witty sou

ways shape shifting. un rosthite. Blood type imp ortant. Must like choco pending some evening one.

User-friendly, software o mized for a romantic, lon relationship. Alienations ep end.

HARD DRIVE, SOFTWARE, ROMANCE

Beta Tester Wanted—Boyfriend 97. User-friendly, software optimized for a romantic, long-term relationship. Processes exercise, conversation, dance, movies, and more. Hosted on good-looking, 40s frame (5′ 7″, 155 lb.), Jewish operating system but Christian compatible. Slim, attractive, boyfriend literate candidates please apply.

Hacker wanted—SWF, 20, seeking shy, cute SWM, computer whiz, 18–28. Don't worry, I don't byte. Trying . . . Connected.

Office Cruise—SWM with Microsoft Office 97. Let's cruise together through Access, Excel, Word, and PowerPoint. Let's create a learning experience as we share and learn together. Call for the itinerary.

LIBRARY OF LOVE

Modern Day Don Quixote battling windmills and enchanters. Beneath the armor lies a tall slender frame, 35+ years of age with a handsome face. He never looks back; only forward, hoping to someday meet Lady Dulcinea. Could she be you?

Searching the 100 Acre Wood— Tigger seeks cuddly, silly, "old" bear (single, fit, 43–50, Pooh variety)! Tigger's 46, bouncy, energetic, vibrant, strawberry blonde, 5′ 6″, does her stoutness exercises regularly and has 2 junior Tiggers 14 and 18. In addition to hunting Heffalumps, thoughtful, caring, perceptive Pooh knows that without love and friendship, the woods can be a very lonely place. Perhaps we could meet over a pot of honey?

Alice Lost in Wonderland chasing white rabbit. No mock turtles or disappearing Cheshire cats. Eat this, drink that, size unimportant. Queen of hearts will approve!

Little Engine That Could . . . I can take care of myself, but can this non-smoking 45 year old Little Engine find a man to go around the track with me? I think I can!!! (No baggage car or large caboose!) Call and toot your whistle!

New to Area, slightly used novel, nice hard cover, cute glossary, in circulation 36 years. Looking for height/weight proportionate F to blow the dust off my cover and run her fingers through my pages. My table of contents includes: successful multi-state business owner, athletic, 6′, 210 lbs., homeowner, recently divorced, with son, antique collector, good at back rubs. My pages will make you laugh, cry, moan, gasp, and you'll want to stay up reading me all night long. My references include: fitness, picnics, biking, cooking, cuddling. I'm best read snuggled in front of a blazing fire or candles, with soft music, bottle of wine, or good movie. I even dance pretty well for an old book.

You Are What You Read: Handsome *Esquire*, 38, 5′ 9″, 165 lbs., seeks alluring petite *Elle*, 30s, for *Time Out*. Me: *NY Times*, *New York*, *Economist*, *Vanity Fair*, *Opera News* at home; *Wall Street Journal*, *Women's Wear Daily* for work. You could be: *Artforum*, *Backstage*, *Gourmet*, *Scientific American*, *Foreign Affairs*. No *Cosmo* girls please. Respond with details.

PUT ME IN, COACH... I'M READY TO PLAY

Hoist the Cup—Attractive avid puckster, 33, seeks adorable SWF who feels awe at the power of an Avalanche! Believe tripping, high-sticking, and checking between partners is detrimental and requires two minutes in the box. Don't get shutout—join me at the blue line for some cake and icing.

Lead Off Batter—needed for well-balanced roster. Left-fielding, self-aware, "Crash Davis" type. Benefits include an attractive stadium with natural turf, loyal, appreciative fans, and passionate, spiritual mascot. Must provide autographs gratis and love kids. Longterm contract negotiable.

Out of Practice Ex-Yankee—
SWF benched too long seeks coach for practice; major league contract possible. Attractive 5′ 8″, dark hair, green eyes, 41. Coach—under 50, conscious, considerate, honest, patient, into snuggling, sailing. Spirited at challenging ladies. Call for tryouts.

Looking for a Starter—not an armchair quarterback. Desire and dedication required for this 5′ 8″, size 12, 31 year old rookie. Please be open to intense one-on-one practices and two-sided press conferences. Level playing field is waiting for you.

Rookie Seeks Same—for franchise history—not just one season. Sports loving, romantic professional with curly red hair (31, single, white female, size 12) needs sincere team mate (6′+, 30–42, single or divorced white male, nonsmoker) to help tackle life's challenging seasons and celebrate all our victories.

Football fever—Seeking tight end to pass time and touch down with Monday Night Football. I am a seasoned DPWF, 33, looking for an enthusiastic team player to move down the field until playoffs.

New freshman on court. Bi black female, new in ball games, never dribbled or shot a free throw. Looking for a good coach to teach me how to shoot a free throw. Only want to play a few quarters. No butch or man-haters.

Fighter Wanted—Pretty SWF, contender, seeks champion boxer/black belt to go 15 rounds, for relationship, knockout, or marriage.

ANCIENTS WANTED

Neolithic Man—Cave-dwelling WM, 33, 5′ 10″, 190 lbs., with small club and more artistic than aggressive instincts seeks new Stone Age woman, clan of the cave bear or other tribe for hunting, gathering, and exploring the S.F. Bay region.

Me Good You Bad—Ugg, grunt, lone white male, grrr, seek, grunt ugg, mate, grrr ugh, ugh 2 grrr evolve with.

Cave Babe!—Tired of hanging out at watering holes with guys. Pretty, prehistoric, San Francisco cave babe, 30-something, fit, uses bones to tone. You should be mid-30's to early 50's, honest, flexible, have dinosaur. Ugh!

Viking wanted—Tall, dark to pillage and plunder neighboring villages. King Stanley's brilliant and lovely daughter will be interviewing Viking candidates, so be prepared.

CONTEMPORARY WARRIORS

SW Male, 40, seeks lifemate to help dig foxholes, make bombs, forage abandoned cities, determine which mutant plants are edible, clean and load machine guns, lay booby traps, and stitch flesh. 'Cause Armageddon won't be any fun to face alone.

Handsome guerrilla fighter, deep in Hollywood jungle. Seeks dark unclassifiable beauty to commemorate his battles with snapshots. Charisma, fearlessness, familiarity with escape trails through the mountains desirable.

FRESH AND SALADLIKE

I have an avocado. If you have a tomato, let's make guacamole. Gourmet cook, age 43, has cabernet to share. Let's toast the town.

Salad spinner, 45-year-old northern celery heart seeks hot tomato for tossed salad; two croutons included. Please leave your telephone number!

Pickleman seeks Izzy. Handsome SWEET SJM who RELISHes life and hasn't SOURed on the idea of love, seeks DILLightful SJF-30's to CURE me of bachelorhood.

Harvest Pumpkin—This positively perfect produce, plucked from a harvest patch, is a simple and pure pleasure that no other fruit can match. 33 years to create a 5′ 5″, 350 lb. work of art. Scarecrow, Lion, Tin Man—Warm this pumpkin's heart.

FULL PLATE ENTRÉE

ISO Grade A Beef—SGWM ISO hot-beef injection, no slimjims or beef jerky need apply. Whoppers w/o cheese only please. Tacos with extra beef and salsa can head for my border.

God, send me an angel, won't tear us apart.

...1, colt-less, educated, ...ssful, attractive, ...t/weight proportionate, ...hy.

...put on our capes and ...s and team up for ad... ...re! To the Batpoles! ...rs, Two-Faces and Cat-...an need not apply.

...le white male seeks ...dly Baywatch wannabe ...knows when to turn it ...nd when to turn it on. ...ired; mouth to mouth ...icitation.

...y 20's woman looking ...gothic man who has an ...ng for the darker things.

...le foundation and at-...ive appearance add to ...uality and charm. Pre-...fy: you are handsome, ...33-41, financially, emo-...lly and physically fit, ...o appreciate!

...llector's item, low main-...nce and some assembly ...red. Act now, and re-...a boomerang demoli-...on free! Hurry! Offer ...ed.

...M, 28, tall, slender ...gs (brown/blue color ...ne). Safe for outdoor ...athletic use. Many ...ehold uses in garden, ...shop, kitchen. Travel ...y (extensively held ...d overseas).

...ear oldprofessional ...ng for match who's 25-...andsome, honest, ma-...and not looking for ...orary source of heat

GWF, 29, avid swimmer ...ing private investigator, ...an who isn't afraid of ...eep end.

dust off my cover and run her fingers through my pages.

Coach—under 50, conscious, considerate, honest, patient, into snuggling, sailing. Spirited at challenging ladies. Call for tryouts

...1949 or 1953. Better like dogs.

Get your hands dirty with this hot young archaeologist looking for an Indiana Jones to excavate my secret passageways. Must have a mind

that glimmering star to capture me in her gravitational pull. One star planet, will orbit you with affection, his molten core will fuel those passions to keep your sparkle shining.

I'm your candidate for

...animated cuddlers to hiber-nate with in the 100 Acre Woods of life.

SM interested in meeting an individual who can surprise me with her unique and of-fensive beauties, not her ex-

sense of humor, Worf's strength, Riker's height, Geordi's intelligence and communicator skills like Picard. I am shapely like Troi.

Robert DeNiro kinda guy. Seeks woman with Green-...wich Village cool. Little

...graduate student, 31. Me: postmodern hipster; English-Literature degree, rockabilly, like waffles. You: must hate hippies, drunks, frozen yo-gurt. Cat: black.

Dashing, 31, 6'3", 180lbs,

...rsourceful repartees, h... ...not hype. Me,yes, flick s... ...tin', tune whistlin', natur... ...flavorful, savvy, fun! y, tr... ...junkie.

Consider dating me! Eve... ...woman I've dated in the ...years has ended up w... ...r former boyfriend! N... ...ls! References availab...

...O Meaningful relation... ...th cute dyke who can ...ir Ford pick-up truck

...rmask, join hands, jum... ...wn, spin around, plung... ...o the pool? Ecstatic ...rposes? I say we do i

...WM, 5'10", 200 poun... ...ack hair, eyes. Seeking ...all, all redhead, young ...ney. I want the bubble ...coated for us with ho... ...days.

...ose men who cuddle ...opes for love are seda... ...their darling's charm ...only have tired arms f... ...ving hugged the cloud... ...ove.

...the prowl for a male ...ot a male line) who's s... ...ate male, 5'7"+, 25-4...

...WM, 36, seeking prett... ...ing SWF, sweetheart... ...eed your pollen. My st... ...ll keep you blooming.

...tite white professiona... ...le, 45, mistrust ing ...unette beauty searchi... ...lion king. Scratching ...ling—all possible. Le... ...a kilt, dance all nigh... ...nt all day.

...rn Violin seeks match ...y for warm harmonic ...counters. Fretwork in ...ites exceptional grac... ...een eyes, auburn hair. ...ument produces melo... ...s, intelligent, witty so...

...boys shape shifting ar... ...osthite. Blood type un... ...portant. Must like drag... ...spending some evening ...alone.

User-friendly, software ir... ...m zed for a romantic, Iq... ...term relationship. Pro...

147 Pound Hunk of un-smoked masculine beef, 5 ft. 7 in., short br/blue, lean but tender, will provide much active energy, also savory for romantic dinners. Looks 35–38 "prime," but aged 47—a steal! ISO similar, cultured, reliable younger chef, max 5 ft. 11 in.

Dinner for Two? I have olive skin, well-formed sourdough buns, avocado smooth thighs, sweet basil breath. I'm sensual, sensitive, gentle, playful, 26, seeking natural, tender, fresh connection with attractive, mature, unconventional twenty-something who enjoys food, art, exercise. Care to taste?

Chili lover seeks hot tomato. Not too spicy, bean there, done that. Must have touch of sweetness. The only pot I use is for cooking chili. OK, so I am an acquired taste. Shall we heat up a batch?

SMOOTH AND CHEESY

Cheesehead—seeking cute little curd for whey out fun! Low fat brands only. Aged 30–38 years. Let's fun-do and put on the Ritz. Soft churned smooth qualities desired.

Bagel seeks cream cheese. Seeking mellow, delectable, low-fat blend, 33–40. This 'n' That bagel is SWJPM, mid-40s, 5′ 10″, 185, scrumptious, all natural with toasty warm smile wanting stick-together relationship.

SWEET AND SUGARY DESSERTS

Smart Cookie wants to crumble in your hands. Cute, low-fat, slightly nutty, 13780 days old, 5′ 9″, good shape, with dough, like kneading. Seeking 28–38 tough cookie with tender heart and unconventional taste. Honest, direct recipe for intimate bite.

Like Ritalin for Chocolate— 31, SW Rocky, somewhat nutty, non-truffling truffle is looking for fudge. Packrat, chock full of Mounds of stimulating Almond Joyous ideas, not candy-coated, whole aspartamed vanilla. We swirl Quick through the Milky Way on dark/white retro/goth Snickering. Hugs and Kisses at Goodbar.

Just desserts—Single white female, angel food cake, 35, 5′ 7″ layers, all nonfat, candles glow when lit, seeks single white male, 6′ layers plus, pound cake, must rise to the occasion. No crumbs please.

Chocolate mousse—
No excess calories, firm texture, sweet, won't melt under extreme heat, large spoon included. Missing flavorsome, low-fat vanilla cream to go on top. Chilled at least 21 years.

Doughgirl seeks Gingerbread man. Fresh, soft, WF, 40+ ISO crisp, younger M to meet mutual kneads. Want cookies.

Hard Shell—Soft Center—Sweet Valentine candy and romance is hidden under a hard shell, this 40 year old SWM will deeply warm your heart and melt in your hand "if" you can see beyond his hard entrepreneurial shell and get to his soft center.

SPICY!

Spice-Racked—I've dated all the Spice Girls, and they turned out to be salt substitutes. Looking for something more to my taste. Can you help me exhaust these "food" analogies? No one under the age of the oldest Hanson.

DRINK OF ME . . .

A Rare Vintage—The complexity and breeding of a fine Bordeaux; the elegance of an exceptional burgundy combined with the youthful exuberance of a Beaujolais Nouveau and the spiciness and depth of a great Zinfandel, attractively bottled, seeking oenphile [*sic*] 25–45.

1956 Vintage—
Romantic SWM seeks a sweet white wine, vintage dated. No screw off tops. Non-acidic, classic bottle shape. Call me and let's get out of the cellar together and breathe.

Some men, like vintage wine, age well. Attractive full-bodied, vigorous, 53, 6′ 6″ man ISO ripe, robust, delicious man, aged 35–45. He would be sparkling, tangy yet sweet, nonsmoker/drug, urban, monogamous. Looking for perfect blend.

Like fine wine—Pale, W, soft, nice bouquet, aged well, 35, sparkling, refined, for first growth, WM who finishes with finesse, 32–45, uncork the possibilities.

Fine Wine: 1956 vintage stored in Gettysburg cellar. Shaken but not opened. Can you open the bottle?

Oddly Described Features and Peculiar Assets

Body Shape

Aykroyd-esque in build

Slightly chunkified

Slightly Rubenesque

Built like a Sherman tank (tough and made to last)

Voluptuous (old-school definition)

Medium thin

Barely full-figured

Plump but I fit through the door

A 1985 thick Oprah Winfrey physique

Linebacker build with gooey cream filling

Bikini-challenged

Semi-short

Non-short

Adult height

Non-Rubenesque

Unfat

Non-fat

Non-spherical (shape)

Mushy core

Legs aren't the only thing I have in abundance

Construction worker build

Hair and Lack Thereof

Nobly bald

Bald with blond hair

John Lithgow haircut

Bleached blonde hair, brunette brain

Not follically impaired

Hasselhoff hair

Curly hair (genetic perm)

Unbald

Fattish hair

Long blond hair like Thor

Sure There Are Blue Eyes, Brown Eyes, Even Irish Eyes but . . .

Bloodstone eyes

Mood eyes

Byzantine eyes

Monet blue eyes

Andy Garcia eyes

"Talking" eyes

Snoopy brown eyes

I wear fake color contacts. Whatever eye color you love, I'll wear.

Facial Features

Jane Seymour nose

British face

Lightly pierced

Head on shoulders

Head screwed on

I have fine "Waspy" facial features

Dark and mesmerizing (Neil Diamond–ish)

[I am] attractive (through squeezed eyelids)

Work and Career

"About to blow-up" as renowed [*sic*]
scholar/author/public intellectual

Published author (available in Barnes & Noble)

Caucasian widow of film president

I am an experienced Toastmaster

Blue-collar professional

Blood donor

I am a writer. I am a psychic.

[I] was Celtic warrior priest in past lives

Own and operate an 800 acre Beefmaster ranch

Planning to be the next Chinese
fast food chain founder

Genuine French baron

Has pilot license (but no plane)

Ex–romance novel model

Former Mr. Jacksonville

Former switchboard operator

Post-College/Pre-Real Life

[I am] corporate-wife type

Screenwriter/proletarian

Airline captain/bus owner

Serious enough to be a lawyer

Dental hygienist, good oral skills

Employed 20 years with major utility company

Jewish-Italian actress perhaps switching to mental health care profession

You would be the boss. Would be open to most demands.

Useful Skills

Comfortable at Monaco black-tie dinners

I can hang at Borders all day
without buying a thing

When I make jokes, people spit out
what they're drinking

Strong bladder

I'm the kind of person who would help a lost dog

Enjoys vocalizing various character voices

Never embarrass women in public

Eclectic intensity developed as
former advertising photographer

Occasional cross-dresser

Can decipher acronyms

Excellent penmanship

Similar to Celebrities

Tom Selleck's age

Tom Cruise look-alike (in a former life)

Terry Bradshaw look-alike

Mary Tyler Moore smile

Trendy (Sarah McLachlan look)

If Mary Tyler Moore were a 33 year old male, he'd be me!

People say I look like Elvis when he was young

People say I resemble "Yanni" (physically not musically)

Cleopatra type

Look like a pint-sized Travolta

I am a cross between James Bond and Galileo

Like Kerouac only sober

Spiritual/Inner Life

Frequently psychic

East Coast morals

Inwardly mobile

Near death experienced

Am open (but not fond of
Weird Al or heavy beards)

Accurate Christian

Enjoys all that God approves

My conversation and/or attendance will
never embarrass your Godliness

Circumstantially tolerant

Fully aware of his God-given majesty

Moody (in a good way)

Mildly Gothic

Recovering radical environmentalist

Fascinating Contradictions

Liberal thinking with conservative look

Classic in future sense

Straight with gay sensibilities

Male lesbian

Clean living in a messy house

Zany in a normal way

Average on the outside but a stud on the inside

WASP in a brown body

Good listener/talkative

Hardbodied, combing the best of
white and blue collar

Hippie in an Armani suit

Jewish culturally, but looks Irish

Family

I have been raised by my mother

I am my daughter's father

My Dad lived to be 106

SWM, 35, with famous dead relatives

Product of good genes and
responsible living

More Assorted Assets and Oddly Described Features

Legally available

Omnivorous reader

Kenny G intolerant

Chihuahua owner

Been to Cuba

Born the same year Chandler
wrote "The Pencil"

Lived in India, Santa Fe, and
Poughkeepsie

I own countless Carpenters videos

In transition down to size 10
but currently a size 14

Ex-European

Successful hippie

Slow-moving

Never misses *The McLaughlin Group* on Sundays
(unless sleeping off a hangover)

BABY, YOU CAN DRIVE MY CAR

Less Than Zero—Low financing or lease with option to buy (not literally), good mpg, four-wheel drive, stick shift (don't get any ideas), anti-lock brakes (no air bags, sorry). Take a test drive and sign on the dotted line, because it's the last model in stock. GWM, tall, thin, early 20's, blond/blue.

For Sale—1968 model white guy. Running on all cylinders, very attractive exterior, a real eye-catcher. Low miles. Runs like new! Driver confident in turns. Perfect for moonlit drives in the country or be-bopping around town on a Saturday night. Not a guzzler. Backfires once in a while, but can be controlled. Once you take a test drive, you'll want to take him home with you. Act fast—this baby won't be on the lot for long. Will even trade for like model. You asked for it, you got it.

1958 Model American Classic, needs lady mechanic. One owner, body in good shape, hazel-colored lights, thick carpeting, radio plays soft classic rock, oldies, humor. Engine recently torn up. Mechanic should have knowledge of Italian, French, bbsing, AANR, TLC ways of making engine purr. Although license [*sic*], experience not necessary.

Hot Rod Wanted—This subcompact guy (5 ft. 6 in. blue, brown, slim) is looking for a hot ride in a masculine machine. Tall, 5 ft. 8 in.+, handsome late model '55 to present with a very well-equipped cockpit is hotly desired. I've driven on the right side of the road for years and am ready for a lane change. Are you? My grade is not cool for oil changes, is yours? If so, don't call Jiffy Lube, call me.

'64 Beetle (low mileage & well maintained) seeks similar vintage (1960–67). French makes (Simca, Citroën, D2CV) a plus. Enjoys swimming (remember Herbie?), regular tune-ups & both urban & wilderness destinations. Turn offs: broken signals, fender benders, & rear-end collisions. Looking for the right model w/ whom to settle into a nice 2-car garage & play "Chitty Chitty Bang Bang."

'51 Special—Buick—One owner, large engine and headers, brown/hazel & tan, a delight to drive, quad stereo, not a gas hog, no smoke, low maintenance, not for sale, trade only, requires protective coating and hand polishing.

Road tested, garage kept, classy. Eye-pleasing exterior, gears shift gracefully from daytime organizer to nighttime prowler. Radio works most stations. Brakes for tubesteaks, lobster tails, and boats. 50, DWF seeks NS fun DWM.

Drivers wanted—Black, mint condition, low miles, good engine. Nice headlights and bumper. SBF, 28.

Rent-A-Wreck—used, comfortable, broken-in, with a high-revving tachometer, many miles to go with good tires and stereo. Real clean and road worthy. Never held children or smoke. Seeking female co-pilot.

Previously Owned Compact—

Classic '47 Leo, original parts, no rust, runs great. Fine for camping, concerts, music fests, clubs, movies, outings, etc. Compact size makes for easy handling/parking, yet room for kids and pets. Sporty model, fun to drive (note: veers to left).

Classic 1964 Mustang—newly Oregon registered, low miles, garage kept. Performs well in city traffic and country cruising with radio tuned to Rock 'n' Roll, Country/Western, or Oldies. Trim body style with warm interior includes empty backseat for kids. Reliable for daily driving and weekend road trips. Looking for classy 50's to 60's late model with clean record and clear title. SWM, 6′ 1″, 160, brown and hazel.

Are you a purple Ferrari?

Custom and top of the line? Needed: well-kept, low mileage, with clean lines and built from 1956–1966. Must be SWM—no 4 cylinders or smoky tail pipes need apply.

p with one bright,
easy to look at, easy
with SWM feathered
(43-55).

lood—This charming
7 seeks the perfect. F
d new lover with lips
gar, "boy meets girl
od, send me an ange
on't tear us apart.

, colt-less, educated,
sful, attractive,
weight proportionat
y.

dust off my cover and run
her fingers through my
pages.

Coach—under 50, conscious,
considerate, honest, patient,
into snuggling, sailing. Spirited at challenging ladies.
Call for targets.

that glimmering star to capture me in her gravitational
pull. One star planet, will
orbit you with affection, his
molten core will fuel those
passions to keep your
sparkle shining.

I'm your candidate for

sense of humor, Worf's
strength, Riker's height,
Geordi's intelligence and
communicator skills like Picard. I am shapely like Troi.

Robert DeNiro kinda guy.
Seeks woman with Green-
wich Village soul. I like

ut on our capes and
and team up for ad
e! To the Batpoles!
, Two-Faces and Cat-
need not apply.

white male seeks
y Baywatch wannabe
ows when to turn it
d when to turn it on.
ed; mouth to mouth
tation.

20's woman looking
othic man who has a
for the darker thing

foundation and at-
e appearance add to
ality and charm. Pre
: you are handsome,
3-41, financially, em
y and physically fit,
appreciate!

ctor's item, low mi
e and some assembly
d. Act now, and re
a boomerang demon
n free! Hurry! Offer

28, tall, slender
s thrown/blue color
). Safe for outdoor
hletic use. Many
old uses in garden,
op, kitchen. Travel
extensively held
overseas).

r oldprofessional
for match who's 2
dsome, honest, ma-
nd not looking for
rary source of heat.

WF, 29, avid swimmer
private investigato
is fishing for a
who isn't afraid of
p end.

Lease Option to Buy—
1968 white convertible coupe, stored too long in cool environment, longing to hug the open road. Call for a test drive, no haggling please.

her former boyfriend! Ne
alls! References availabl

50 Meaningful relationsh
with cute dyke who can re
pair Ford pick-up truck.

Unmask, join hands, turn
down, spin around, plunge
into the pool? Ecstatic lit
porpoises? I say we do it!

SWM, 5'10", 200 pound
black hair, eyes. Seeking
small, all redhead, young
honey. I want the bubble w
be coated for us with hon
always.

Those men who cuddle
whores for love are sedate
by their darling's charms
only have tired arms fro
having hugged the clouds
above.

On the prowl for a male lie
(not a male line) who's sir
white male, 5'7"+, 23-40

SWM, 36, seeking pretty
young SWF, sweetheart.
Need your pollen. My stin
will keep you blooming.

Petite white professional
male, 45, nonsmoking
brunette beauty searching
for lion king. Scratching a
biting—all possible. Lust
for a kill, dance all night,
hunt all day.

Rare Violin seeks matchin
bow for warm harmonious
encounters. Fretwork in-
cludes exceptional curves
green eyes, auburn hair. Ir
strument produces melodi
ous, intelligent, witty soun

y shape shifting
rosthite. Blood type unim
portant. Must like dragon
spending some evening
alone.

User-friendly, software onl
nized for a romantic, long
erm relationship. Proces

1949 or 1953. Better like
dogs.

Get your hands dirty with
this hot young archaeologist
looking for an Indiana Jones
to excavate my secret pas-
sageways. Must have a mind

more than succeed either
animated cuddlers to hiber-
nate with in the 100 Acre
Woods of life.

SM interested in meeting an
individual who can surprise
me with her unique and of-
fensive beauties, not her ex-

graduate student, 31. Me:
postmodern hipster, English-
Literature degree, rockabilly,
like waffles. You: must hate
hippies, drunks, frozen yo-
gurt. Cat: black.

Dashing, 31, 6'3", 180lbs,

1949 two seat roadster, reconditioned but very fast. Seeks skilled driver capable of revving my engine. Experienced drivers only to take me for a test drive up the coast or through the country and show me your curves. DJM, non-smoking.

For lease with option: Sleek, 1950s Alfa Romeo, one owner, low mileage, good body, runs great DJF, petite and darn cute, seeks 1948–1959 Porsche, mint condition, plush interior SJPM for a cruisin' LTR.

1970 American Stock, well-groomed, low mileage, clean, reliable, runs like new. Stands 5′ 8″, 175 pounds, sporting new hi-tops for smooth ride. Seeks: 1965 to 1975 truck for off-roading.

Late 30s roadster, beige, long classic style, perfect for high Wintry, Gatsby gentleman with firm Christian values, time, and tender loving care. ISO highway to heaven.

THE ALWAYS DEPENDABLE KNIGHT IN SHINING ARMOR

Dented Armor—Tall, handsome knight, 29, seeks same to plan our own crusade. I'm tired of slaying dragons and pointless jousting. If you're into college sports, music, movies, and intelligent conversation and you're not a damsel in distress, call my castle immediately.

Damsel wanted—Gallant knight seeks maiden fair to rescue from her despair. Attractive, romantic, funny, artistic SWPM with White-Knight complex seeks soulmate to rescue and adore. Well-known in the realms for his ability to slay dragons and mend broken hearts. He still searches for his true love. Legend has it that she is 18–30 yrs., slight of build, quixotic, refined, yet impishly playful. Legend also tells of her fiery hair and skin of pure alabaster. A reward of 300 drekmars will be awarded to anyone w/ information leading to the union of this enchantress and loyal Cavalier.

ISO Princess—31 year old knight in shining armor, with a few dents from dragons disguised as princesses. On a quest for a true princess.

Young, handsome, Scottish prince, trapped in castle. Von Locksaline, cursed by royalty, isolated in popularity, driven by creativity. Seeks: princess to come rescue me. True-heart, Brave-heart, Lone-heart.

Chivalry can never die as long as I draw breath. White knight seeks black queen to save from the dragons of solitude. If your heart longs for magic, cry out! And I may storm the tower for thee.

THE BUSINESS OF LOVE

Bad credit? No credit? Bankruptcy? Who cares? Instant credit when you open your heart! Economy-sized attractive GWM, 6′ 1″, 350, offers Equal Opportunity. If your interest rate is rising, make the investment. Call today!

Excellent Opportunity— Girlfriend wanted: experience preferred, great emotional benefits package, excellent chance for advancement. DWM, 45, tall, successful, friendly, seeks humorous, sensuous female. Partnership opportunity available. All qualified applicants considered.

od, send me an angel,
on't tear us apart.

, colt-less, educated,
sful, attractive,
weight proportionate
y.

ut on our capes and
and team up for ad-
e! To the Batpoles!
. Two-Faces and Cat-
i need not apply.

white male seeks
y Baywatch wannabe
nows when to turn it
d when to turn it on.
ed: mouth to mouth
itation.

20's woman looking
othic man who has a
for the darker things.

foundation and at-
e appearance add to
ality and charm. Pre-
: you are handsome,
3-41, financially, emo-
y and physically fit,
appreciate!

ector's item, low main
e and some assembly
ed. Act now, and re-
boomerang demon-
n free! Hurry! Offer

28, tall, slender
s (brown/blue color
e). Safe for outdoor
hletic use. Many
hold uses in garden,
hop, kitchen. Travel
(extensively field
overseas).

r old professional
g for match who's 25
ndsome, honest, ma-
nd not looking for
rary source of heat

WF, 29, avid swimmer
g is fishing for a
n who isn't afraid of
ep end.

dust off my cover and run
her fingers through my
pages.

Coach—under 50, conscious,
considerate, honest, patient,
into snuggling, sailing. Spirited at challenging ladies.

that glimmering star to capture me in her gravitational
pull. One star planet, will
orbit you with affection, his-
molten core will fuel those
passions to keep your
sparkle shining.

sense of humor, Worf's
strength, Riker's height,
Geordi's intelligence and
communicator skills like Picard. I am shapely like Troi.

Robert DeNiro kinda guy.
Seeks woman with Green-

Personal loan DWM, 5′ 1″, 170 pounds, healthy, versatile seeks worthy WF for approved transactions. Weekly, monthly, and long term plans available. Interest earned daily.

1949 or 1953. Better like
dogs.

Get your hands dirty with
this hot young archaeologist
looking for an Indiana Jones
to excavate my secret pas-
sageways. Must have a mind

animated cuddlers to hiber-
nate with in the 100 Acre
Woods of life.

SM interested in meeting an
individual who can surprise
me with her unique and of-
fensive beauties not her ex-

graduate student, 31. Me:
postmodern hipster, English-
Literature degree, rockabilly,
like waffles. You: must hate
hippies, drunks, frozen yo-
gurt. Cat: black.

Dashing, 31, 6'9", 180lbs

POSTMODERN AND SELF-AWARE

[Witty, attention-grabbing first sentence.] SWM, 28 years, [assurance of attractiveness], writer/editor, guitarist [string of positive alliterative adjectives], recent NYC transplant seeks sophisticated-yet-unpretentious SWPF, 22–32 years for [slightly oblique reference to desire for companionship]. My passions include biking, cooking, DeLillo, Doonesbury, and molesting small animals. Oh, and irony.

Me?! Advertise?! No way! Remember, I'm a warm, sensitive, tall, dark, handsome Englishman. I can find vibrant, creative, tall, beautiful, non-mainstream women whenever I want. So please, leave me alone!

Bold catchy headline followed by 30 words or less describing available, desirable gentleman. Conclude with vague, yet hip reference to San Francisco's post-modern urban culture. SWPM, 37. Call for details.

Me: 22, slightly weird SM. You: slightly weird too. Age not important but with love of books and nature. I have much better things to do than think up a witty ad to sell myself—so just take a chance and call.

Don't read this ad!!! It's unusual, the stranger who wrote it is probably unusual too and you have so much success meeting normal guys the normal way.

Help! I'm trapped in a personal ad!! Me: 28, bright, funny, quirky, overeducated, and artistic. I'm not a dork! How did I get in this box?

Sorry but they've only allotted me forty words to convey to you the depths of my soul. Oh dear! Now it's only twenty-three words. I mean seventeen! No, fourteen! This is terrible! Now I have only eight left! What shall

WEARY OF THE PROCESS

Blah Blah Blah! Blah, blah, blah, blah, 6′, blah, blah, blah, blah, blah, blah, blah, blah, blah, NS, Fit, 48.

Good-Looking, Tall blonde, 34, blah blah blah (smart but no dark roots) is searching for you, blah blah blah (no moustache or gold chains).

Blah Blah Blah—
Professional, blah, blah, blah, blah, white male, blah, blah, blah, 32, blah, blah, blah, nice looking, blah, blah, blah, seeks blah, blah, blah, fun, blah, blah, blah, energetic, blah, blah, blah, creative, blah, blah, blah, female.

Love. Love, love.

Absolute.

Box 6131—To the 57 men who answered my ad, I am now a lesbian.

SHORTEST ADS

Available!

Fhsdjfsfhksjh

Looking. Ask me.

Wanted. Mr. Right.

I want a lover.

Small, stubborn, selfish, and rude.
Like movies.

FYI, SWPF ISO SWM, ASAP

Wanted: One warm woman.

Absolutely perfect man seeks same.

Nothing Seeks Nothing. No expectations.

Eligible bachelor seeks Ms. Right.

Hi, go ahead and give me a call.

I'm a minimalist, so call me already!

Real man seeks real woman. No Democrats, smokers OK.

Single Japanese female, 20 years, ISO WM, 20–40 years. I like ice cream.

TOYS AND GAMES

Queen of hearts seeks joker, 22–26, for fair game. Please be one of a kind and look good in a suit.

New Beanie Baby—Slim the Cute Man. Date of birth, June 13, 1951, looks 35. Heart tag in mint condition. Dimensions: 5′ 7″, 155, non-smoker. Looking to Ty the knot with Girl Beanie under 40, height/weight proportionate.

Are You Gaym?—Winning in the game of Life? Does romance seem like a Trivial Pursuit? How about a little Twister? If you don't own Boardwalk, that's okay. Just no Baltic Avenue, please! Playing piece size not important. Preferred players: GWMs, 5′ 8″ or taller, dark hair, light eyes a plus! This player: handsome, GHM, 5′ 6″, Playing to Win!

STAR SIGNS

Capricorn wanted.

Professional WM, 43, 5′ 11″, 170 lbs. non-smoker, Virgo wants to contact slender, professional WF, non-smoker born January 5–19 of 1953, January 1–6 of 1955, or January 6–19 of 1961.

Velvet Glove Libran— Looking for Aquarius man born February 4th, 12th, or 16th, especially in the year 1949 or 1953. Better like dogs. Me: sweet, blond hair, blue eyes, 5′ 3″, 125 lbs., scholar, artist, musician, writer; creative, funny, original, and lonely.

Somewhere in time—Could enduring spirit based, playful intimacy come more easily with certain astrological alignments? If your birthday is 5-29-68, 5-30-68, 6-4-68, 6-10-68, 6-11-68, 10-5-58, 10-6-58, 10-10-58, 10-11-58, 6-7-52, 6-8-52, or 6-9-52, we'll find out.

Unfortunate Typos

If you are out there, please **waive**, I'm willing to make a crash landing.

Age [is] **irreverent**.

No **vises** please.

Stop **the** smell of roses.

Don't even bother to play with this **gamey** chick.

Vegetarian **tenancies** preferred.

Your ethically unimportant.

If I **peaked** your curiosity, please give me a call.

Who likes the same **acclivities**

ISO an assertive male for some interesting **tomes**.

[I love] **crouchless** panties.

We will be spelunking, partying, **repelling**, shooting pool.

[Seeking woman who is] **unfridged**

If you are a honest, hard-working man looking for a woman to **steel** your heart . . . then I am the one.

Dating is Hell! **Expect** with me . . .

Grisly Adams look-a-like

I am a serious songwriter in the pop-folk **vain.**

Close-**crapped** hair

Ralph **Nator** Fan

Must be empathetic, **articualte**

Collage graduate

Sexy **brained** beauty

. . . Who knows her Bukowski from her **Nobokov.**

Educater, 45 . . .

[Am pursuing] dual career as actor/**playwrite**

Favorite artist, **Cezann**

Romeo, Romeo **Where for out** thou Romeo

Sofisticated yet down to earth

Kafka **reding** college graduate

open-minded, **ceribral**

Sexy Harvard **philosoppher**

Read **Thereau** in the morning

[I'm as] **smart** as a tack.

SCHOOL OF LOVE

Move to the head of the class! Date a teacher, every schoolboy's fantasy! DWF, 46, petite (5′ red/blue), lover of life, with great sense of humor, seeks non-smoking, well-balanced, intelligent man, 35–55. Who knows what we can learn from one another?

Head of the Class looking for teacher's pet . . . must attend all classes. Willing to learn, must be good listener, capable of passing hard test: LTR, in the books. Lessons of the heart, classroom on-site. Sign-up enrollments now being taken for students aged 35–49.

Jock Scholar needed to fill athletic, academic, and social quota at well-established 25 year-old institution. Good SAT scores, sports ability, and BMOC good looks could land you a scholarship at the U of Me. Must also be able to share off-campus housing and TLC with one year old mascot. Come play for us. No oxymorons please.

...dust off my cover and run her fingers through my pages.

Coach—under 50, conscious, considerate, honest, patient, into snuggling, sailing. Spirited at challenging ladies. Call for tryouts...

...that glimmering star to capture me in her gravitational pull. One star planet, will orbit you with affection, his molten core will fuel those passions to keep your sparkle shining.
I'm your candidate for...

...sense of humor, Worf's strength, Riker's height, Geordi's intelligence and communicator skills like Picard. I am shapely like Troi.
Robert DeNiro kinda guy. Seeks woman with Green-...

...ship with one bright, ...y, easy to look at, easy ...e with SWM feathered ...

...blood—This charming ...37 seeks the perfect ...and new lover with lips ...sugar, "boy meets girl" ...God, send me an ange... won't tear us apart.

...41, colt-less, educated, ...essful, attractive, ...ht/weight proportionat... thy.

...s put on our capes and ...ls and team up for ad...ure! To the Batpoles! ...rs, Two-Faces and Cat... ...an need not apply.

...le white male seeks ...dly Baywatch wannab... ...knows when to turn it ...and when to turn it on... ...ired; mouth to mouth ...scitation.

...y 20's woman looking ...a gothic man who has ...ng for the darker thing...

...le foundation and at... ...tive appearance add to ...quality and charm. Pre...ify; you are handsome, ...33-41, financially, em...ally and physically fit ...o appreciate!

...llector's item, low ma...nce and some assembl...ired. Act now, and re...e a boomerang demoli...tion free! Hurry! Offer...ed.

...M, 28, tall, slender ...ngs (brown/blue color ...me). Safe for outdoor ...athletic use. Many ...ehold uses in garden, ...shop, kitchen. Travel ...y (extensively hold ...d overseas).

...ear oldprofessional ...ing for match who's 2... ...handsome, honest, ma... ...and not looking for ...orary source of heat.

GWF, 29, avid swimm... ...ling private investigat... ...er, is fishing for a ...an who isn't afraid of ...eep end.

ASSORTED OCCUPATIONS

Schedule an appointment. Independent SWPF 37 yrs., N/S, pleasantly coiffed, no preservatives ISO curling up with chemically-free SWPM, over 30 years. Permanent relationship only. No quick trims or blow-drys.

...her former boyfriend! ...ails! References availa...

...50 Meaningful relation... ...with cute dyke who car... ...pair Ford pick-up truck...

...Unmask, join hands, ju... ...down, spin around, plu... ...into the pool? Ecstatic ...porpoises? I say we do...

...SWM, 5'10", 200 pou... ...black hair, eyes. Seekin... ...small, all redhead, your ...honey. I want the bubbl... ...be coated for us with h...always.

...Those men who cuddle ...whores for love are sed... ...zy their darling's charm... ...only have tired armshaving hugged the clou...above.

...On the prowl for a male ...(not a male line) who's ...white male, 5'7"+, 25-4...

...SWM, 36, seeking pret... ...young SWF, sweetheart... ...Need your pollen. My s... ...will keep you blooming.

...Petite white profession... ...male, 45, nonsmoking ...brunette beauty searchi... ...for lion king. Scratching ...biting—all possible. Let... ...for a kill, dance all nigh... ...und all day.

...Rare Violin seeks match... ...bow for warm harmonic ...encounters. Fretwork in... ...cludes exceptional curv... ...green eyes, auburn hair, ...strument produces melo... ...ous, intelligent, witty so... ...mance, shape shifting fo...

...User-friendly, software ...mized for a romantic, lo... ...term relationship. Proce...

...1949 or 1953. Better like dogs.

Get your hands dirty with this hot young archaeologist looking for an Indiana Jones to excavate my secret pas-sageways. Must have a mind...

...more than half-seed other animated cuddlers to hiber-nate with in the 100 Acre Woods of life.

SM interested in meeting an individual who can surprise me with her unique and of-fensive beauties, not her ex-...

...graduate student, 31. Me: postmodern hipster, English Literature degree, rockabilly, like waffles. You: must hate hippies, drunks, frozen yo-gurt. Cat: black.

Dashing, 31, 6'3", 180lbs,...

Wayward apostrophe's . . .

. . . drive me nuts! Copy editor, 33, seeks fellow word nerd, 28–38, to help punctuate her free time with movies, dog walks, dining, and more. Extra points for good spelling!

Live wire ISO positive connection. Artist/teacher/mom with two grounded charges ISO low-resistance intensity without power surges, short circuits, blown fuses. You: 40s, incandescent smile, magnetic personality, bright. You & I: Generators and transformers.

ship with one bright, any, easy to look at, easy be with SWM feathered end (43-55).

dust off my cover and run her fingers through my pages.

Coach–under 50, conscious, considerate, honest, patient, into snuggling, sailing. Spirited at challenging ladies. Call for tryouts.

that glimmering star to capture me in her gravitational pull. One star planet, will orbit you with affection, his molten core will fuel those passions to keep your sparkle shining.

I'm your candidate for

sense of humor, Worf's strength, Riker's height, Geordi's intelligence and communicator skills like Picard. I am shapely like Troi.

Robert DeNiro l-inda guy. Seeks woman with Green-wich Village cool. Little

e blood–This charming n 37 seeks the perfect brand new lover with lips e sugar, "boy meets girl" ur God, send me an angel e won't tear us apart.

41, colt-less, educated cessful, attractive, ight/weight proportionate lthy.

's put on our capes and vls and team up for adture! To the Batpoles! ers, Two-Faces and Cat-man need not apply.

gle white male seeks ndly Baywatch wannabe o knows when to turn it and when to turn it on. quired: mouth to mouth uscitation.

ly 20's woman looking a gothic man who has a ling for the darker thing

ble foundation and atctive appearance add to quality and charm. Prefy: you are handsome, , 33-41, financially, em nally and physically fit, to appreciate!

ollector's item, low mai ance and some assembly uired. Act now, and reve a boomerang demon-ation free! Hurry! Offer ited.

M, 28, tall, slender ings (brown/blue color eme). Safe for outdoor athletic use. Many sehold uses in garden, rkshop, kitchen. Travel dy (extensively field ed overseas).

year old professional king for match who's 2 handsome, honest, ma-e and not looking for porary source of heat

GWF, 29, avid swimm ding private investigato er, is fishing for a man who isn't afraid of deep end.

er former boyfriend! ails! References avail

0 Meaningful relatio with cute dyke who ca hair Ford pick-up truc

Unmask, join hands, ju down, spin around, plu nto the pool? Ecstatic porpoises? I say we do

SWM, 5'10", 200 pou lack hair, eyes. Seekir mall, all redhead, you honey. I want the bubb e coated for us with h always.

hose men who cuddle whores for love are se y their darling's char only have tired arms having hugged the cou above.

n the prowl for a mal not a male line) who is white male, 5'7"+, 25-

WM, 36, seel ing pre oung SWF, sweethear Need your pollen. My will keep you blooming

Petite white professor nale, 45, nonsmoking runette beauty search or lion king. Scratchir iting—all possible. Le or a kill, dance all nig unt all day.

Rare Violin seeks mat ow for warm harmon ncounters. Fretwork i cludes exceptional cur reen eyes, auburn hai trument produces me us, intelligent, witty s

njoys shape shiftum rostbite. Blood type u ortant. Must like dra pending some evening alone.

User-friendly, softwa mized for a romantic,

1949 or 1953. Better like dogs.

Get your hands dirty with this hot young archaeologist looking for an Indiana Jones to excavate my secret passageways. Must have a mind

animated cuddlers to hibernate with in the 100 Acre Woods of life.

SM interested in meeting an individual who can surprise me with her unique and offensive beauties, not her ex

graduate student, 31. Me: postmodern hipster, English-Literature degree, rockabilly, like waffles. You: must hate hippies, drunks, frozen yogurt. Cat: black.

Dashing 31, 6'3", 190lbs

Dig Me—Get your hands dirty with this hot young archaeologist looking for an Indiana Jones to excavate my secret passageways. Must have a mind for adventure and a penchant for the exotic. Don't forget your bullwhip.

ALL ABOARD!

Antique tugboat built in 1942, a few dents and dings, engine runs great, hull undergoing overhaul, loves calm open seas, but can weather most storms, captain charting new course.

Surrounding column fragments:

...ship with one bright, ...ny, easy to look at, easy ...be with SWM feathered ...end (43-55).

...ke blood–This charming ...n 37 seeks the perfect F ...brand new lover with lips ...e sugar, "boy meets girl ...ir God, send me an ange ...e won't tear us apart.

...41, colt-less, educated, ...ccessful, attractive, ...ght/weight proportionat ...althy.

...'s put on our capes and ...vis and team up for ad ...ture! To the Batpoles! ...ers, Two-Faces and Cat ...man need not apply.

...gle white male seeks ...endly Baywatch wannab ...o knows when to turn it ...and when to turn it on. ...quired: mouth to mouth ...uscitation.

...rly 20's woman looking ...a gothic man who has ...ling for the darker thing

...ble foundation and at ...ctive appearance add to ...quality and charm. Pre ...alify: you are handsome, ...33–41, financially, em ...ially and physically fit, ...to appreciate!

...ollector's item, low ma ...ance and some assembl ...uired. Act now, and re ...e a boomerang demon ...ation free! Hurry! Offer ...ited.

...M, 28, tall, slender ...lings (brown/blue color ...eme). Safe for outdoor ...l athletic use. Many ...sehold uses in garden, ...kshop, kitchen. Travel ...dy (extensively field ...ted overseas).

...year old professional ...king for match who's 25 ...handsome, honest, ma ...e and not looking for ...mporary source of heat

...s GWF, 29, avid swimmer, ...iding private investigato ...cer, is fishing for a ...man who isn't afraid of ...deep end.

...dust on my cover and run ...her fingers through my ...pages. Coach–under 50, conscious, ...considerate, honest, patient, ...into snuggling, sailing. Spir ...ited at challenging ladies. ...Call for tryouts.

1949 or 1953. Better like dogs. Get your hands dirty with this hot young archaeologist looking for an Indiana Jones to excavate my secret pas ...sageways. Must have a mind

...that glimmering star to cap ...ture me in her gravitational ...pull. One star planet, will ...orbit you with affection, his ...molten core will fuel those ...passions to keep your ...sparkle shining.

I'm your candidate for

animated cuddlers to hiber ...nate with in the 100 Acre ...Woods of life. SM interested in meeting an individual who can surprise me with her unique and of ...fensive beauties, not her ex

...sense of humor, Worf's ...strength, Riker's height, ...Geordi's intelligence and ...communicator skills like Pi ...card. I am shapely like Troi.

Robert DeNiro kinda guy. ...Seeks woman with Green ...wich Village cool. Little

graduate student, 31. Me: ...postmodern hipster, English ...Literature degree, rockabilly, ...like waffles. You: must hate ...hippies, drunkes, frozen yo ...gurt. Cat: black.

Dashing, 31, 6'3", 180lbs,

...er former boyfriend! ...ails! References avai

...50 Meaningful relatio ...with cute dyke who ca ...air Ford pick-up tru

...Unmask, join hands, j ...down, spin around, plu ...nto the pool? Ecstati ...porpoises? I say we do

...BWM, 5'10", 200 po ...black hair, eyes. Seeki ...small, all redhead, yo ...honey. I want the bub ...e coated for us with ...always.

...hose men who cuddle ...whores for love are se ...by their darling's char ...only have tired arms ...having hugged the clo ...bove.

...n the prowl for a mate ...(not a male line) who's ...white male, 5'7"+, 25

...SWM, 36, seeking pre ...young SWF, sweetheart ...Need your pollen. My ...will keep you blooming

...Pxtite white professio ...male, 45, nonsmoking ...brunette beauty searc ...er lion king. Scratchin ...biting—all possible. L ...or a kill, dance all nig ...hunt all day.

...Rare Violin seeks mat ...bow for warm harmon ...encounters. Fretwork i ...ludes exceptional car ...reen eyes, auburn hai ...trument produces me ...ous, intelligent, witty s

...njoys shape shifting ...rostbite. Blood type u ...portant. Must like dra ...pending some evening ...alone.

...User-friendly, software ...mized for a romantic, ...erm relationship. Pro

Save the Titanic! WPF sinking fast, due to lack of fun and adventure! Seeking tall male to rescue me, who is between 40–55, with romantic life jacket to spare.

Frequent flyer seeking first class home life. Personalized service expected and will be returned. Have upgrade coupons, but haven't found the right flight.

Hello! Welcome to African American Air Lines. Tickets for today's flight to Europe, to meet a European/Latin husband, are on sale. All potential masculine(s) should be age 25–45, 5 ft.10 in.+, physically fit, equipped and well prepared to fly, no excess baggage tolerated! Versatile, single, monogamous men issued boarding date passes. This handsome mancraft has logged only 34 flight miles, has 6 ft. of cabin height, weight of 168 lbs., and a caring, atmospheric personality to make one feel very comfortable. A must for the athletic type passenger. Come fly the mahogany skies!! Tickets not sold to game players or bar flies.

LOVE IN SPACE

Terran Conquest—Single white female from Mars seeks brainy guy for Terran conquest. Bring weapons.

Warm planet wandering through space, searching for that glimmering star to capture me in her gravitational pull. One star planet, will orbit you with affection, his molten core will fuel those passions to keep your sparkle shining. Divorced white male, 5′ 11″, 42.

I'M A CONTENDER!

Elect Me! Ladies, I'm your candidate for higher office with a lifetime of commitment. SWM, professional, 5′ 10″, with blond hair and blue eyes, seeks female for her vote of confidence. Cast your ballot for me. Call this ad!

Campaigning for a running mate for a winning ticket. The polls show this WM, 36, has a strong lead for his personality, integrity, and good looks. This candidate's profile is 5′ 7″, 160 lb., br/br, good shape. The party's diverse platform agenda includes outdoors, travel, music & movies, restaurants. ISO a landslide election with a WM, 30–38, handsome, mainstream, masculine, outgoing, honest, HIV-neg. Seeking re-election for the long term. No time for corruption or scandals. The polls close soon, so cast your vote now.

Unfortunate Grammar

Professional mom of 49

. . . For random romps through the yellowed leaves and snow

Playful woman with out children

[I am] committable

Financially successful with hair

Great butt, legs in Brooklyn

Possibility of a relationship, up to 27 years

Let's break the wind! [This was an ad seeking a fellow motorcyclist.]

ALLITERATE ME!

Airline attendant, amiable, attractive, affectionate, accessible, available, amble anywhere, articulate, adjusted, alert, albeit adventurous, adaptable, answers 5′ 3″, 50's S/DWF, height/weight proportionate.

Experience everything—Emphatically enormously enthusiastic European. Eclectic educator. Energetic, effervescent. Entertaining and wildly diverse professor.

Extraordinary, expansive, ex-urbanite exceeds expectations. Extends exceptional ex-option for existential examination. Experience exhilarating exhibitions of excellence; expect expert exhortations, exuberant expressions, exquisite excapades, extended external explorations; exotic exploits extra. Ex-medic, expatriate, ex-lingual, ex-lover, ex-loner, exposed as SWM ex-40's, 6′ 2″, ex-blonde.

Fantastic find: single, Jewish female, 5′ of fair feminine face, form, and figure; 55, physically fit, full faculties, felicitous, fair-minded family therapist seeks 50ish fellow traveler, farsighted, fascinating, funny, far-out, or fun-loving flame for 50/50 forever after. Foreign born fine. Phone!

Frosty February Felicity this feminine yet funky, festive yet fortitudinous, frolicsome, flashy, fantastic at fifty, SWPF, seeking fit feeling-filled, friendly SWPM, with finesse for flavorful friendship and frivolous foozling.

The FM Dial—fantastic, funny, friendly, fascinating, fearless, fashionable, freckled, faithful, festive, fetching, first-born, flower growing, SWF, 44. Seeks mirthful, memorable, mindful, multifaceted, mannered, musical, mellow, mysterious, monogamous, mountain loving, SWM, 39–48, non-smoking, no drugs, for friendship and possible marr . . . long-term relationship.

Fit, fun, not yet forty female finds funny, friendly, forty-ish fellas fabulous. Fone!

Luscious, libidinous, logical, luxuriantly large (not lean), licentious lady who loves levity looking for lingual, loving lullabies and loving liaisons. No loathsome lotharios or lazars!

Lovely lass likely to light up your life, Libra, lighthearted, liberal, ladylike. Looking to lure logical, lucky like-minded, lively, legitimate, and lucrative Lancelot, 50–60, to land lasting laughter. No lemons, lushes, or louses.

with one bright,
easy to look at, easy
with SWM feathered
(43-55).

lood–This charming
7 seeks the perfect F
d new lover with lips
igar, "boy meets girl"
od, send me an ange
on't tear us apart.

I, colt-less, educated,
stful, attractive,
weight proportionate
y.

out on our capes and
and team up for ad-
e! To the Batpoles!
s, Two-Faces and Cat-
n need not apply.

white male seeks
ly Baywatch wannabe
nows when to turn it
d when to turn it on.
red; mouth to mouth
itation.

20's woman looking
gothic man who has a
for the darker thing

foundation and at-
e appearance add to
ality and charm. Pre-
y: you are handsome,
3-41, financially, emo
y and physically fit,
appreciate!

ector's item, low ma
ce and some assembly
ed. Act now, and re-
a boomerang demon-
n free! Hurry! Offer
.

, 28, tall, slender
s (brown/blue color
e). Safe for outdoor
hletic use. Many
old uses in garden,
hop, kitchen. Travel
(extensively held
overseas).

r oldprofessional
g for match who's 2
ndsome, honest, ma-
and not looking for
rary source of heat.

WF, 29, avid swimme
g private investigato
is fishing for a
who isn't afraid of
ep end.

dust off my cover and run
her fingers through my
pages.

Coach–under 50, conscious,
considerate, honest, patient,
into snuggling, sailing. Spirited at challenging ladies.
Call for targets.

that glimmering star to capture me in her gravitational
pull. One star planet, will
orbit you with affection, his
molten core will fuel those
passions to keep your
sparkle shining.

I'm your candidate for

sense of humor, Worf's
strength, Riker's height,
Geordi's intelligence and
communicator skills like Picard. I am shapely like Troi.

Robert DeNiro l-nda guy.
Seeks woman with Green-
wich Village soul. Little

Mmmm, Mmmm, Mmmm—
Marriage minded monoga-
mous male must meet mate.
Music, movies, motorcycles,
museums, mountains,
massage, metaphysics,
markets, mischief, and
merrymaking. SWPM, 6′,
blond/blue ISO n/s SWF, ISO
LTR & possibly children.
Alliteration optional.

er former boyfriend! Ne
ails! References availab

50 Meaningful relationsl
with cute dyke who can n
air Ford pick-up truck.

Unmask, join hands, jum
own, spin around, plung
nto the pool? Ecstatic l
orpoises? I say we do it,

SWM, 5'10", 200 pound
black hair, eyes. Seeking
mall, all redhead, young
oney. I want the bubble
e coated fur us with hor
always.

hose men who cuddle
whores for love are sedat
y their darling's charms
only have tired arms fr
aving hugged the clouds
above.

n the prowl for a male li
not a male line) who's si
white male, 5'7"+, 25-40

SWM, 36, seel ing pretty
oung SWF, sweetheart.
Need your pollen. My stir
ill keep you blooming.

Petite white professional
male, 45, nonsmoking
rinette beauty searching
or lion king. Scratching
ting—all possible. Let'
r a kill, dance all night,
unt all day.

Rare Violin seeks matchir
ow for warm harmoniou
ncounters. Fretwork in-
ludes exceptional curves
reen eyes, auburn hair. I
trument produces melod
us, intelligent, witty sour
Enjoys shape shifting an
rostbite. Blood type impo
ortant. Must like dragor
pending some evening
lone.

User-friendly, software of
mized for a romantic, lor
erm relationship. Proces

1949 or 1953. Better like
dogs.

Get your hands dirty with
this hot young archaeologist
looking for an Indiana Jones
to excavate my secret pas-
sageways. Must have a mind

animated cuddlers to hiber-
nate with in the 100 Acre
Woods of life.

SM interested in meeting an
individual who can surprise
me with her unique and of-
fensive beauties, not her ex-

graduate student, 31. Me:
postmodern hipster, English-
Literature student, rockabilly,
like waffles. You: must hate
hippies, clowns, frozen yo-
gurt. Cat: black.

Dashing, 31, 6'3", 180lbs,

Today's show is brought to you by the letter *P*: petite, pretty, pert. Polished, progressive. People-oriented, peripatetic, polyglot (Pan-Asian). Passionate, pensive, practical, poetic. Paradoxical. Perceptive, perspicacious, patient. Peculiar, 31 y.o., 5 ft. 2 in., SWF looking for potential longterm partner. Asian language/studies/background a plus. Poor penmanship no problem.

Surreal siren, 29, seeks swarthy, spicy sinner, 30–35, with super-sucker style and sparkplug personality for swing, spaghetti, Sartre, and sacrilegious soul squeeze.

easy to look at, easy to SWM feathered (43-55).

lood–This charming 7 seeks the perfect. F d new lover with lips gar, "boy meets girl" od, send me an ange on't tear us apart.

s, colt-less, educated, sful, attractive, weight proportionat y.

but on our capes and and team up for ad e! To the Batpoles! , Two-Faces and Cat n need not apply.

white male seeks y Baywatch wannabe nows when to turn it d when to turn it on. ed: mouth to mouth itation.

20's woman looking othic man who has for the darker thing

foundation and at e appearance add to ality and charm. Pre r: you are handsome, 3-41, financially, emo y and physically fit, appreciate!

ctor's item, low mai e and some assembl ed. Act now, and re a boomerang demon n free! Hurry! Offer

28, tall, slender s (brown/blue color e). Safe for outdoor hletic use. Many old uses in garden, op, kitchen. Travel extensively field overseas).

r oldprofessional g for match who's 2 ndsome, honest, ma d not looking for rary source of heat

WF, 29, avid swimmer g private investigato is fishing for a who isn't afraid of p end.

st in Wonderland

her fingers through my pages.

Coach–under 50, conscious, considerate, honest, patient, into snuggling, sailing. Spir ited at challenging ladies. Call for tryouts

that glimmering star to cap ture me in her gravitational pull. One star planet, will orbit you with affection, his molten core will fuel those passions to keep your sparkle shining.

I'm your candidate for

1949 or 1953. Better like dogs.

Get your hands dirty with this hot young archaeologist looking for an Indiana Jones to excavate my secret pas sageways. Must have a mind for adventure and a pen

animated cuddlers to hiber nate with in the 100 Acre Woods of life.

SM interested in meeting an individual who can surprise me with her unique and of fensive beauties, not her ex treme and unaccountable

sense of humor, won't strength, Riker's height, Geordi's intelligence and communicator skills like Pi card. I am shapely like Troi.

Robert DeNiro kinda guy. Seeks woman with Green wich Village cool. Little

graduate student, 31. Me: postmodern hipster, English Literature degree, rockabilly like waffles. You: must hate hippies, drunks, frozen yo gurt. Cat: black.

Dashing, 31, 6'3", 180lbs, blue eyes. You are 23-30

her former boyfriend! Ne ails! References availabl

50 Meaningful relations with cute dyke who can r air Ford pick-up truck.

Unmask, join hands, jum down, spin around, plung nto the pool? Ecstatic th orpoises? I say we do it

SWM, 5'10", 200 pound lack hair, eyes. Seeking mall, all redhead, young honey. I want the bubble e coated for us with hon always.

Those men who cuddle whores for love are seda y their darling's charms only have tired arms fr aving hugged the clouds above.

On the prowl for a male li not a male line) who's si white male, 5'7"+, 25-40

SWM, 36, seeking pretty young SWF, sweetheart. Need your pollen. My sti will keep you blooming.

Petite white professional male, 45, nonsmoking brunette beauty searching or lion king. Scratching iting – all possible. Let's or a kill, dance all night, unt all day.

Rare Violin seeks matchin bow for warm harmonious ncounters. Fretwork in ludes exceptional curves reen eyes, auburn hair. I trument produces melod us, intelligent, with soun

njoys shape shifting an rostbite. Blood type unin ortant. Must like dragon pending some evening lone.

User-friendly, software op nized for a romantic, lon erm relationship. Proces

Sensuous, successful, scholar— Sharp-witted, slow-handed, safe, satisfying, secure, stable, scrupled, studious, sporting, sometimes sarcastic, sociopolitically sentient, socially skilled, serious, suasive, sagacious, scientific, skeptical, SWNSNRJPM, 6′ 3″, 190 lbs., 39, seeks scintillating, stimulating, sane, sensible, sincere, sweet, sunny, sanguine, sportive, sometimes saucy, stylish, somewhat svelte, sinuously shapely, stunning, sizzling, steamy siren of substance.

Visionary Vixen—Verve, veracious, vivacious, vivid vision, vivifying, visceral volition, vegetarian, vehement, voluble, vulpine virtuoso, vatic valiant, vantage vying verse libre vibe vibe . . . va va voom! Vroom, vroom!

Wet, Wild, Wonderful women waterskiers with wit/wisdom who wanna waterski with well-meaning, willful wooers—wanted.

HORN TOOTERS

JFK Jr. look-a-like some say, but I think better

Hollywood insider with celebrity friends and VIP guest privileges at nightclubs . . . you provide transportation

---

Ex San Francisco 49er

L.A. music executive in town for the holidays

TV talk show host and producer

Television executive . . . gets invited to Academy Awards, Super Bowl, Sundance, Cannes, Broadway, etc.

In famous rock band, tired of groupies

Former Ford model

Widowed white 53 year old, with body of 30 year old and libido of 18 year old

---

I love tight sweaters and short skirts because I look good in them

ROMANCE IS NEXT TO GODLINESS

One Promise Keeper—

Morally sound woman of God, 35, praying for similar man, to share life with Christ together. Romans 8:28.

Christian—I'm white, 42, 5′ 10″, 175 lbs., no children. If the following verses mean something to you: Deuteronomy 6:5, Proverbs 19:14, and Ephesians 5:21–33, I'm interested in hearing from you. You: preferably childless, between 32–43, animal lover a big plus.

hip with one bright, y, easy to look at, easy with SWM feathered d (43–55).

blood—This charming 37 seeks the perfect new lover with lips sugar, "boy meets girl God, send me an ange won't tear us apart.

1, colt-less, educated, ssful, attractive, nt/weight proportionat hy.

put on our capes and s and team up for ad-ure! To the Batpoles! rs, Two-Faces and Cat-an need not apply.

e white male seeks dly Baywatch wannabe knows when to turn it nd when to turn it on ired: mouth to mouth citation.

20's woman looking gothic man who has ng for the darker thing

e foundation and at-ive appearance add to uality and charm. Pre fy: you are handsome, 33–41, financially, emo lly and physically fit, appreciate!

lector's item, low ma ce and some assembl red. Act now, and re a boomerang demon on free! Hurry! Offer ed.

1, 28, tall, slender gs (brown/blue color ne). Safe for outdoor thletic use. Many ehold uses in garden, shop, kitchen. Travel textensively field d overseas).

ar oldprofessional ng for match who's 2 andsome, honest, ma-and not looking for orary source of heat

GWF, 29, avid swimme ng private investigato r, is fishing for a an who isn't afraid of eep end.

dust off my cover and run her fingers through my pages.

Coach—under 50, conscious, considerate, honest, patient, into snuggling, sailing. Spir-ited at challenging ladies. Call for tryouts.

I'm your candidate for

1949 or 1953. Better like dogs.

Get your hands dirty with this hot young archaeologist looking for an Indiana Jones to excavate my secret pas-sageways. Must have a mind

that glimmering star to cap-ture me in her gravitational pull. One star planet, will orbit you with affection, his molten core will fuel those passions to keep your sparkle shining.

animated cuddlers to hiber-nate with in the 100 Acre Woods of life.

SM interested in meeting an individual who can surprise me with her unique and of-fensive beauties, not her ex-

sense of humor, Worf's strength, Riker's height, Geordi's intelligence and communicator skills like Pi-card. I am shapely like Troi.

Robert DeNiro kinda guy. Seeks woman with Green-wich Village cool. Little

graduate student, 31. Me: postmodern hipster, English-Literature degree, rockabilly, like waffles. You: must hate hippies, drunks, frozen yo-gurt. Cat: black.

Dashing, 31, 6′3″, 180lbs

her former boyfriend! N ails! References availa

SO Meaningful relation with cute dyke who can pair Ford pick-up truck

Unmask, join hands, down, spin around, plun nto the pool? Ecstatic porpoises? I say we do i

SWM, 5′10″, 200 poun black hair, eyes. Seeking small, all redhead, youn oney. I want the bubble e coated for us with ho always.

Those men who cuddle whores for love are seda by their darling's charm only have tired arms fr aving hugged the cloud above.

On the prowl for a male not a male line) who's s white male, 5′7″+, 25-4

SWM, 36, seeking prett young SWF, sweetheart. Need your pollen. My st will keep you blooming.

Petite white professiona male, 45, nonsmoking brunette beauty searchi or lion king. Scratching iting—all possible. Let or a kill, dance all night unt all day.

Rare Violin seeks match ow for warm harmonio ncounters. Fretwork in cludes exceptional curve green eyes, auburn hai strument produces melo us, intelligent, witty sou

Enjoys shape shifting a rostbite. Blood type un ortant. Must like drag pending some evening alone.

User-friendly, software o nized for a romantic, lo erm relationship

God Gave Mike Tyson another chance. So give me a chance, open your heart, let me in. We've been blessed in many ways by God, we forget to acknowledge and give thanks to God, we only think of our wants, humans are so selfish. Yes, I say this to all, SBF, attractive shapely God's property. Seeking tall, attractive, built gentleman of any origin for companionship. "Ask God about me, and he'll tell you I'm nice and good."

Recently liberated priest, 5′ 10″, 178 lbs., looking for action. Needs love, companion, and dancing machine with S/DW/A/HF, height/weight proportionate who needs a blessing. I won't make you say any rosaries, but you might, Hail Mary!

Leaving My Monastery. SW Monk, 5′ 11″, 25 years old, brown hair, green eyes, and a great Irish accent. I enjoy fine conversation, fine dining, and bad jokes. You should be between 21 and 30, athletic, tolerant of bad jokes, ready to be pampered (I give great neck rubs), and able to handle an ex-monk returning to the world.

NOW PLAYING

Jumpin' Jack Flash—Desperately Seeking Susan for *True Romance*. *My Girl*, *She's the One* who *Dances with Wolves*, while *Driving Miss Daisy*, but isn't *Sleeping with the Enemy*.

Going to *Extreme Measures* not to find *The Usual Suspects*. Are you my *Glimmer Man*? Maybe I'm your *Spitfire Grill*. We: 40s and worth *Two Days in the Valley* for *Long Kiss Goodnight*. Call for showtimes.

Tom Cruise look-alike seeks co-star for *Risky Business. Far and Away*, the best catch here, this *Rain Man* offers downpours of devotion and *Days* (and nights) *of Thunder. Top Guns* need only reply.

Reality Bites and so do I . . . sometimes! I'm tired of *Flirting with Disaster* in *Zero Effect* relationships, but absolutely groove on that Ben Stiller type. Call to hear *Something About Mary* (that's me) if you're super curious.

DATE MOVIES

James Bond—British Secret Agent seeks Ms. Moneypenny for international adventures. James is 31, educated, charming, cover is successful entrepreneur. Has all Q's toys. Moneypenny is 28–32 Bond girl with license to thrill. Prepare to be stirred not shaken.

Cornelius seeks his Zira for rendezvous in Ape City. SWPM, 27 desires SWPF, 22–29 for fun, friendship, possible LTR.

C-3P0 seeks R2—You're my only hope. Sad droid needs to find counterpart in order to restore peace to the galaxy. I must find my mate so we can rendezvous in the city of the clouds and we can both feel the force.

Indiana Jones, Jr.—Dear old dad was an adventurer, and so am I. 6′ 2″, 210 lbs., single white male, seeks woman to treasure and hunt treasure with. We will explore, tempt fate, and live large. Must be fit, fearless, and have own whip.

"Dorothy," bright, winsome, shapely, genuine, 37, seeks brainy, kind-hearted, and courageous companion for Yellow Brick Road adventures. Eventually, I'd like munchkins and a home in Oz with educated affectionate wizard.

Friend of Dorothy—GWM wizard ISO Toto man looking for love under the rainbow. I could provide brain, heart, and nerve to someone in the fellow pick mode. You should be reasonably intelligent, personally sensitive, and financially independent. Please no straw men, tin men, or pussy cats need apply.

READY FOR MY CLOSE-UP

Lottery of Love—Leading lady sought for role of lifetime. Scenes to include scintillating dialogue, dining, dancing, outdoor activities, improvisation. Must be intelligent, sharp, with sense of humor and joie de vivre. Producing, directing credit to be shared with SJM.

Hooray for Hollywood— Mature male lead seeks experienced yet marketable ingenue to co-star in new romantic, action, sci-fi, adventure, comedy blockbuster to begin production this spring. Must look good in fur bikini and must do own stunts.

Auditions for Co-Star. Qualifications: 45–62, HWP, have a playful nature with good sense of timing for quick ad-lib lines; you read lines clearly with true feeling. Experience as a co-star in a role that is finished and reads "The End" would be helpful and yet not necessary. This will be a part like you have never played before. Be willing to travel and be on location for some of the movie, "This Marvelous Life." A current passport is good to have. Be financially independent, as this role pays in other ways besides money—some pay being: love, mutual response, and romance. Bonus: If you are cast as the co-lead, expect a loving, committed relationship with the Oscar winning co-writer, co-producer, co-director, co-choreographer, and co-star!!! Call or write casting office today!

ASSORTED ENTERTAINERS

Magician seeking lovely assistant. Tricks include: pulling rabbits out of hats (like the world needs more rabbits), sawing assistant in half (I'm working on the putting-assistant-back-together thing), levitation (down to just 3 strings now). Magician: 38, handsome, short, trim, muscular, very bright, very funny (helps when tricks fail). Note: not a real magician, though I play one in this ad.

Sleek young sheik seeks an exotic belly dancer for evenings full of wiggles and jiggles. Please keep arms and legs inside ride at all times, loose articles are easily lost.

PLEASE BE ALL THESE PEOPLE

To qualify for this section, the advertiser had to demand that the respondent be a combination of at least three (often astonishingly disparate!) people.

Tall, Slender, Beautiful SWF, 48, creative, professional, seeks easygoing, creative n/s S/DWM, 43–50 with the heart of *Mother Teresa*, the courageous dash of *Errol Flynn*, and the wit of *Bill Murray*.

Athena Seeks Adonis—
Fair-haired maiden seeks single WM with the wallet of *Trump*, a *Highlander* bod, and the genius of *Einstein*. Renaissance applicants welcome. 35–45, non-smoker/no drugs. Bring your sword.

Afrikan warrior, 37, 6′ 4″, requires fertile goddess for homestead, 35 to 45, *Jamaica Kincaid* descriptiveness, *Toni Morrison* strength, *Maya Angelou* bravery, *Coltrane* spirit. Seeking friend, expressive lover, soulful partner, and soulmate.

Current Boyfriends: Frasier and Seinfeld. Past Lovers: Jimmy Buffett, Frank Sinatra, and Billy Joel. Seeking *Larry King, David Letterman, Ted Koppel* type for interview over dinner and drinks.

Absolutely adorable— Redhead, height/weight proportionate, blue eyes, very sexy, bright, funny, considerate, and forthright. Seeking single white professional male 28–40, who is as macho as *John Wayne*, as sensitive as *Jimmy Stewart*, sophisticated as *Cary Grant*, and of course, *James Dean* cool.

Beautiful Brainiac—
Dazzling SWF, long blonde hair, sapphire eyes, delicate body (5′ 4″, 107 lbs.), 34, sexy and smart. Cross between a Hooters waitress and a rocket scientist. Seeking special guy, 30–45, with *Tom Cruise*'s looks, *Jim Carrey*'s personality, and *Einstein*'s mind.

Crazy and poetic . . . a hint of *Dalí* insanity, creative as *Basquiat*, the mysterious aura of *Warhol*, and as sexy as *Morrison*. SHF ISO SWM 28–35, open, real secure in most aspects, somehow normal, not bothered by small issues, and not afraid of life. Art, music, dance, interracial relationships?

SSS & More S's—Smiley, sensuous, and sexy. A mind for business and a body for sin. Seeking a cross between *Richard Gere*, *Robert Redford*, and *Pierce Brosnan* in one package.

Looking for Love—Are you ready for a sensual combination of Xena, Cybill, and Dax? I'm 5′ 7″, 135 lbs., degreed professional. You are a romantic combination of *Captain Jake Sisko*, *Nash Bridges*, and *Tim Allen*. Tall dark and professional. Let's cyber chat.

PLEASE BE ALL THESE IMAGINARY PEOPLE AND "BEINGS" . . .

A Dash Of—S Latin woman seeking SWM, 32–38, weigh at least 180 lbs. You have to have these following ingredients: a dash of *William the Braveheart*, a dash of *Cyrano de Bergerac*, a dash of *Willy Wonka*, a dash of *Bugs Bunny*. If you are this passionate male with a romantic and creative soul, please call.

Pooh Bear—GWM, 33 (br/gry 240 lbs. 6′ 2″ beard/hairy), cuddly and snuggly but stuffed with more than fluff seeks other animated cuddlers to hibernate with in the 100 Acre Wood of life. Like, this Willy Nilly Ol' Bear you must possess *Tigger*'s aggressiveness, *Owl*'s honesty, *Rabbit*'s wit, *Eeyore*'s sincerity, *Kanga*'s lovingness, *Roo*'s innocence, and *Christopher Robin*'s imagination. Can you be the author in the next chapter of this Pooh's life?

Warp Drive Asian—36, 5', 100 lbs., road trips, 70's music, computers, light smoker/light drinker. Seeking tall, stocky, professional WM with *Data*'s sense of humor, *Worf*'s strength, *Riker*'s height, *Geordi*'s intelligence, and communicator skills like *Picard*. I am shapely like Troi.

with one bright, easy to look at, easy with SWM feathered (43-55).

food—This charming 7 seeks the perfect F nd new lover with lips gay: "boy meets girl" God, send me an ange on't tear us apart.

, colt-less, educated, sful, attractive, weight proportionate y.

out on our capes and and team up for ad- e! To the Batpoles! , Two-Faces and Cat- n need not apply.

white male seeks y Baywatch wannabe nows when to turn it d when to turn it on. red, mouth to mouth litation.

20's woman looking othic man who has a for the darker thing

foundation and at- e appearance add to ality and charm. Pre r: you are handsome, 3-41, financially, emo y and physically fit, appreciate!

ector's item, low mai ce and some assembl ed. Act now, and re- a boomerang demon- in free! Hurry! Offer J.

, 28, tall, slender s (brown/blue color e). Safe for outdoor hletic use. Many nold uses in garden, hop, kitchen. Travel (extensively field overseas).

ir oldprofessional g for match who's 25 ndsome, honest, ma- nd not looking for rary source of heat

WF, 29, avid swimmer, g private investigato is fishing for a who isn't afraid of ep end.

dust off my cover and run her fingers through my pages.

Coach—under 50, conscious, considerate, honest, patient, into snuggling, sailing. Spir- ited at challenging ladies. Call for tryouts.

that glimmering star to cap- ture me in her gravitational pull. One star planet, will orbit you with affection, his molten core will fuel those passions to keep your sparkle shining.

I'm your candidate for

sense of humor, Worf's strength, Riker's height, Geordi's intelligence and communicator skills like Pi- card. I am shapely like Troi.

Robert DeNiro kinda guy. Seeks woman with Green- wich Village cool. Little

1949 or 1953. Better like dogs.

Get your hands dirty with this hot young archaeologist looking for an Indiana Jones to excavate my secret pas- sageways. Must have a mind

animated cuddlers to hiber- nate with in the 100 Acre Woods of life.

SM interested in meeting an individual who can surprise me with her unique and of- fensive beauties, not her ex-

graduate student, 31. Me: postmodern hipster, English- Literature degree, rockabilly, like waffles. You: must hate hippies, drunks, frozen yo- gurt. Cat: black.

Dashing, 31, 6'3", 180lbs,

er former boyfriend! Ne ails! References availabl

50 Meaningful relationsh ith cute dyke who can r pair Ford pick-up truck.

Unmask, join hands, jum own, spin around, plunge nto the pool? Ecstatic porpoises? I say we do it

SWM, 5'10", 200 pound lack hair, eyes. Seeking small, all redhead, young oney. I want the bubble e coated for us with hon always.

Those men who cuddle whores for love are sedat y their darling's charms only have tired arms fro aving hugged the clouds above.

On the prowl for a male li not a male line) who's si white male, 5'7"+, 25-40

SWM, 36, seeking pretty oung SWF, sweetheart. Need your pollen. My stir will keep you blooming.

Petite white professional male, 45, nonsmoking. runette beauty searching or lion king. Scratching a iting — all possible. Let's or a kill, dance all night, unt all day.

Rare Violin seeks matchin ow for warm harmoniou encounters. Fretwork in- ludes exceptional curves reen eyes, auburn hair. In strument produces melod ous, intelligent, witty sou

Enjoy shape shifting un rostbite. Blood type uni ortant. Must like dragor pending some evening lone.

User-friendly, software of nized for a romantic, lon erm relationship. Proce

PLEASE BE ALL THESE NEIGHBORHOODS . . .

I'll Take Manhattan—Handsome, New Yorker in D.C., warm, masculine, passionate, funny, courageous, slightly upscale, definitely street smart, incurably romantic, 5 ft. 9 in., 43, trim, Al Pacino, Robert De Niro kinda guy. Seeks woman with *Greenwich Village* cool, *Little Italy* passion, *Lady Liberty* spirit, *Broadway* taste, *Empire State Building* heart.

Details Perhaps Best Left out of Ad . . .

Soon to be divorced (not at my request) . . .

Divorce almost final

Recently survived two-timing gold digger

Just broke up with my girlfriend, yet another train wreck in romance

Ad composed by my ex-wife

The boxers that my ex gave me now have gaping holes in them.

All of my ex-girlfriends' mothers have thought I was cool.

Both my younger exes vouch for my credentials.

Accused of murdering my ex but never formally charged

Caught her cheating, time to pay her back

Been called "thug"

They call me O.J.

Not a felon, what more do you want?

Recently returned from extended federal holiday

Strong Black Man presently finds himself being held under political circumstances.

Dateless for 9 years

Have not had a relationship since September 1995

I've had lots of dates, but not many repeat performances.

But, I really need a date for my son's April wedding.

Seeking a like-minded loner

Loner by choice

No longer angry, please call.

My nights off are Thursday and Friday.

Willing to go out anytime except during Monday Night Nitro

I work till the middle of the night. I work every weekend and holiday.

Short on spare time

Wants steady relationship, but not to last longer than one year

My therapist helped me write this.

Past history of excessive fear of new things

"Flew over the cuckoo's nest" years ago

Like meeting people, but have trouble getting along with them

Shy and confused by women

Women have always thought I was wonderful but couldn't take my craziness.

At times I'm moody, kinda flaky, and lacking in diplomacy.

I'd still prefer someone young and thin, but at 41, will compromise.

I live with a callous [sic] on my heart. Can you help me remove it?

[I am] ideal for someone who is not too picky.

I'm not really as pathetic as I sound.

You don't have to be interesting or entertaining just caring.

I'm very shy and introverted, looking for someone who's patient and doesn't mind a challenge.

I will take of you in a married life.

Stopped fearing marriage ten years ago

Spent much time learning why I've failed at marriage

I've mastered lovemaking—would now like partner.

On rebound from career setbacks

Can't think of a single thing I like about this town

Would like to meet at McDonald's or whatever

My Alabama accent seems to put women off.

Delights in the freedom of living out of my R.V.

Come live like the Unabomber

Seeking F who can enjoy life on a budget

I live the kind of life they make movies about. Need material for the next scene.

I am someone who enjoys watching a scary movie one night and taking a romantic moonlit walk the next.

Banned from most tennis courts

Ruled by my Golden Retriever

My cats told me to get a life.

Interests include necrophilia (just kidding)

Well-spoken when sober

Still drink (preferably single malt) and don't get fired as much as I used to

If it works out, you'll have to promise not to tell my friends we met this way.

A COUPLE OF ENTICING OFFERS—

Long hair and beard— local musician looking for romance. Gotta live the blues to sing the blues.

The surrounding newspaper-style personal ads (partially legible):

r God, send me an angel, won't tear us apart.

41, coil-less, educated, cessful, attractive, ght/weight proportionate, lthy.

's put on our capes and uls and team up for adture! To the Batpoles! ers, Two-Faces and Cat nan need not apply.

gle white male seeks ndly Baywatch wannabe o knows when to turn it and when to turn it on. quired: mouth to mouth uscitation.

rly 20's woman looking a gothic man who has an ling for the darker things

ible foundation and active appearance add to quality and charm. Prealify: you are handsome, , 33-41, financially, emonally and physically fit, to appreciate!

collector's item, low maintance and some assembly quired. Act now, and reve a boomerang demonation free! Hurry! Offer lted.

/M, 28, tall, slender lings (brown/blue color eme). Safe for outdoor d athletic use. Many usehold uses in garden, rkshop, kitchen. Travel dy (extensively held ted overseas).

year old professional aking for match who's 25 handsome, honest, mae and not looking for nporary source of heat

s GWF, 29, avid swimmer ddling private investigator, cer, is fishing for a man who isn't afraid of deep end.

1949 or 1953. Better like dogs.

Get your hands dirty with this hot young archaeologist looking for an Indiana Jones to excavate my secret passageways. Must have a mind

animated cuddlers to hibernate with in the 100 Acre Woods of life.

SM interested in meeting an individual who can surprise me with her unique and offensive beauties, not her ex-

graduate student, 31. Me: postmodern hipster, English-Literature degree, rockabilly, like waffles. You: must hate hippies, drunks, frozen yogurt. Cat: black.

Dashing, 31, 6'3", 180lbs,

sense of humor, Worf's strength, Riker's height, Geordi's intelligence and communicator skills like Picard. I am shapely like Troi.

Robert DeNiro kinda guy. Seeks woman with Green-

I'm your candidate for

that glimmering star to capture me in her gravitational pull. One star planet, will orbit you with affection, his molten core will fuel those passions to keep your sparkle shining.

Coach—under 50, conscious, considerate, honest, patient, into smuggling, sailing. Spirited at challenging ladies.

dust off my cover and run her fingers through my pages.

Alchemist, shaman, Coyote, 50 in 2000 seeking women, conscious, caring, creative women for (1) music, (2) world travel and chess club, (3) holistic convalescent care, (4) possible harem. This is somewhere between a job offer and a marriage proposal. Blessed be.

nip with one bright, y, easy to look at, easy e with SWM feathered d (43-55).

blood—This charming 37 seeks the perfect F and new lover with lips sugar, "boy meets girl God, send me an ange won't tear us apart.

41, colt-less, educated, essful, attractive, nt/weight proportionat chy.

s put on our capes and s and team up for ad- re! To the Batpoles! rs, Two-Faces and Cat an need not apply.

le white male seeks dly Baywatch wannab knows when to turn it nd when to turn it on, iired: mouth to mouth scitation.

/ 20's woman looking gothic man who has ng for the darker thing

le foundation and at- ive appearance add to uality and charm. Pre fy: you are handsome 33-41, financially, em lly and physically fit, o appreciate!

lector's item; low ma ice and some assembl red: Act now, and re- a boomerang demon lon free! Hurry! Offe ed.

M, 28, tall, slender gs (brown/blue color ne). Safe for outdoor athletic use. Many ehold uses in garden, shop, kitchen. Travel y (extensively field d overseas).

ear oldprofessional ng for match who's 2 andsome, honest, ma and not looking for orary source of heat

GWF, 29, avid swimm ing private investigato ing for a an who isn't afraid of eep end.

dust off my cover and run her fingers through my pages.

Coach—under 50, conscious, considerate, honest, patient, into snuggling, sailing. Spir- ited at challenging ladies. Call for tryouts

1949 or 1953. Better like dogs.

Get your hands dirty with this hot young archaeologist looking for an Indiana Jones to excavate my secret pas- sageways. Must have a mind

that glimmering star to cap- ture me in her gravitational pull. One star planet, will orbit you with affection, his molten core will fuel those passions to keep your sparkle shining.

I'm your candidate for

animated cuddlers to hiber- nate with in the 100 Acre Woods of life.

SM interested in meeting an individual who can surprise me with her unique and of- fensive beauties, not her ex-

sense of humor, Worf's strength, Riker's height, Geordi's intelligence and communicator skills like Pi- card. I am shapely like Troi.

Robert DeNiro kinda guy. Seeks woman with Green- wich Village cool. Little

graduate student, 31. Me: postmodern hipster, English- Literature degree, rockabilly, like waffles. You: must hate hippies, drunks, frozen yo- gurt. Cat: black.

Dashing, 31, 6'3", 180lbs,

her former boyfriend! N alls! References availa

50 Meaningful relation with cute dyke who can nair Ford pick-up truck

Unmask, join hands, pu down, spin around, plun nto the pool? Ecstatic orpoises? I say we do

SWM, 5'10", 200 poun black hair, eyes. Seekin small, all redhead, youn noney. I want the bubble oe coated for us with he always.

Those men who cuddle whores for love are sed y their darling's charm only have tired arms t aving hugged the clou above.

On the prowl for a mate not a male line! who's white male, 5'7"+, 25-4

SWM, 36, seeking pretty young SWF, sweetheart. Need your patien. My st vill keep you blooming.

Petite white professiona male, 45, nonsmoking orunette beauty searchin or lion king. Scratching iting—all possible, Let or a kill, dance all nigh unt all day.

Rare Violin seeks match ow for warm harmonio encounters. Fretwork in ludes exceptional curve green eyes, auburn hair, trument produces melo us, intelligent, witty sou njoys shape shifting an rostbite. Blood type un portant. Must like cha spending some evening alone.

User-friendly, software p iized for a romantic, lc erm relationship. Proce

MISSED CONNECTIONS, PASSING GLANCES, CROSSED SIGNALS, AND I SAW YOU

(Ads edited to preserve anonymity.)

Todd Rundgren concert 8/28. You were with your mom. I asked if she forced you into listening to Todd. You said, "No, just Chicago."

Halloween—You: black dress and painted face. We met at a party in Adams Morgan. I was the Pez Dispenser.

Halloween Night: Our eyes met. You: dressed casual, very handsome. Me: well, I had a screwdriver through my head. I hope we find each other.

You: gorgeous woman browsing soundtracks wearing Polo T-shirt. I was opposite you in an Alb shirt. Allergies prevented me from saying anything.

We were both waiting for bus. Talked about rats. Want to go out sometime. Am anxiously awaiting your response.

Home Depot—You: red shirt, name sewn on, white hat, glasses, light hair. I had blue cap, gray shirt, glasses. We passed in lumber. Details which will haunt me till you call.

Alligator Lounge—To the fine blonde waitress in shiny black pants. I'd like to meet you. I sat by myself writing. I wore an old hat. You gave me a flat Coke and a smile.

Lucky Supermarket—New Year's Eve, You: tinfoil in express lane. Me: spinach three aisles over. You crossed the street and disappeared. I am what I am; who are you?

Marlene: Met you at the Elephant Room on your birthday about a year ago. Let me prove I'm not gay.

I SAW YOU (CRIMES, ACCIDENTS, AND CAR CRASHES):

Trouble Prevented a Love Connection

Tempe Jail, Sunday, October 20. We spoke briefly before doing 24 hours. You blonde female, me brown hair and beard. If you're not married and not in love, call!

Special Inmate ISO sister in miniskirt with friend who came close to inmate bus June 6, 1996 outside Manhattan Criminal Court, please write.

You know who you are. We met, I hit your car, you never called. I've reconsidered your offer. Please call.

Department of Motor Vehicles. Talked briefly while you waited to pay ticket. Co-worker embarrassed us both. Want to apologize. Me: dark complexion with striped shirt, jeans, and shades. You: Good-looking, with a personality.

Jury Duty—We talked briefly while waiting in jury lounge. You could be Sandra Bullock's sister. Fellow jurors called me "Mr. Juror #30." Care to exchange depositions?

"They towed my car!" You hoped the rest of my day went better. I hoped you were single, are you?

Kicking Myself: Searching for "G." We met on Sept. 25 on the "T" during the pipe bomb scare. Didn't get your number.

I SAW YOU (ILLNESS AND TRAUMA):

Lovesick and Sorry

Emergency room, Monday: You were with two friends, one with a cut foot. I was there for stitches in hand. You're so fine, mellow and dignified. Can I meet you?

Police officer, near Capitol Building. I had just been in a bicycle accident and asked you where I could clean up. Left note next day. Call if interested.

I was the knee injury you triaged late Sunday night . . . those green eyes of yours have haunted my thoughts ever since. Dinner possible?

You: wearing one of those ugly hospital gowns that open in the back. Me: Trying to stay awake with a big book on my lap. You asked me what I was reading. Ulysses. Wanna explain it to me?

PROMISES

(Some ads come with promised bonus prizes.)

$500 Swiss Army watch is yours if you fit the bill as my boyfriend.

Free lesson on my 1889 Columbia high wheel bike

Extra beer if you speak Portuguese

If fun, free dental care possible.

I'll make you ramen noodles.

We'll share Hawaii frequently.

LOVING BY NUMBER

Be able to name one of the quad cities

Can name at least 3 bands on Matador

Can ID 80's tunes in 3 notes

[You must be able to] name at least three of Rome's seven hills without looking.

You can play the opening chords to 50 songs on the guitar.

You can't name more than five kinds of coffee.

SPECIAL REQUESTS

Couriers especially encouraged

Seeking men who are in fact men

Seeks man of many parts

To incorporate bodybuilding or sculpting with law studies

To see films (non-explosive)

Looking for flight attendant type

Prefer women born in other states

up with one bright, easy to look at, easy with SWM feathered (43-55).

blood—This charming 37 seeks the perfect F nd new lover with lips ugar "boy meets girl" Gori, send me an ange won't tear us apart.

1, colt-less, educated, ssful, attractive, t/weight proportionat y.

put on our capes and and team up for ad-re! To the Batpoles! s, Two-Faces and Cat-an need not apply.

e white male seeks lly Baywatch wannab nows when to turn it d when to turn it on. red: mouth to mouth citation.

20's woman looking gothic man who has a g for the darker thing

e foundation and at-ve appearance add to uality and charm. Pre y: you are handsome, 3-41, financially, ema ly and physically fit, appreciate!

lector's item, low mai ce and some assembl red. Act now, and re-a boomerang demon-n free! Hurry! Offer d.

, 26, tall, slender s (brown/blue color ne). Safe for outdoor thletic use. Many hold uses in garden, shop, kitchen, Travel (extensively field overseas).

ar oldprofessional ng for match who's 2 andsome, honest, ma-nd not looking for rary source of heat

SWF, 29, avid swimmi ng private investigato ; is fishing for a n who isn't afraid of ep end.

dust off my cover and run her fingers through my pages.

Coach—under 50, conscious, considerate, honest, patient, into snuggling, sailing. Spir-ited at challenging ladies. Call for tryouts.

that glimmering star to cap-ture me in her gravitational pull. One star planet, will orbit you with affection, his molten core will fuel those passions to keep your sparkle shining.

I'm your candidate for

sense of humor, Worf's strength, Riker's height, Geordi's intelligence and communicator skills like Pi-card. I am shapely like Troi.

Robert DeNiro kinda guy. Seeks woman with Green-wich Village cool. Little

1949 or 1953. Better like dogs.

Get your hands dirty with this hot young archaeologist looking for an Indiana Jones to excavate my secret pas-sageways. Must have a mind

animated cuddlers to hiber-nate with in the 100 Acre Woods of life.

SM interested in meeting an individual who can surprise me with her unique and of-fensive beauties, not her ex-

graduate student, 31. Me: postmodern hipster, English-Literature degree, rockabilly, like waffles. You: must hate hippies, drunks, frozen yo-gurt. Cat: black.

Dashing, 31, 6'3", 180lbs,

er former boyfriend! Ne alls! References availab

SO Meaningful relations with cute dyke who can hair Ford pick-up truck

Unmask, join hands, jum down, spin around, plung into the pool? Ecstatic porpoises? I say we do it

SWM, 5'10", 200 pound black hair, eyes. Seeking small, all redhead, young honey. I want the bubble be coated for us with hor always.

Those men who cuddle whores for love are seda y their darling's charms only have tired arms fr aving hugged the clouds above.

On the prowl for a mate I not a male line) who's sh white male, 5'7"+, 25-40

SWM, 36, seeking pretty young SWF, sweetheart. Need your pollen. My sti will keep you blooming.

Petite white professional male, 45, nonsmoking brunette beauty searchin or lion king. Scratching biting – all possible. Let's or a hill, dance all night, hunt all day.

Rare Violin seeks matchi now for warm harmonio encounters. Fretwork in ludes exceptional curves green eyes, auburn hair. I trument produces melod pro, intelligent, witty sou njoys share shifting and rostitute. Blood type unin ortant. Must like dragoi pending some evening lone.

User-friendly, software o nized for a romantic, lo erm relationship. Procee

Into exploring other sides of conscious-
ness through tribal-ambient sounds

Looking for a man who dreams of playing
a theremin

Large, calming hands a plus

Would like a man with a big round belly,
like a Sumo wrestler

Seeks Jane Fonda/Ted Turner relationship

If Conan O'Brien were a lawyer, he'd
be my ideal man.

Refer to me as "Thor," God of Thunder

dust off my cover and run
her fingers through my
pages.
Coach–under 50, conscious,
considerate, honest, patient,
into snuggling, sailing. Spirited at challenging ladies.
Call for tryouts.

that glimmering star to capture me in her gravitational
pull. One star planet, will
orbit you with affection, his
molten core will fuel those
passions to keep your
sparkle shining.
I'm your candidate for

sense of humor, Worf's
strength, Riker's height,
Geordi's intelligence and
communicator skills like Picard. I am shapely like Troi.
Robert DeNiro kinda guy.
Seeks woman with Green-
wich Village cool. Little

r God, send me an angel,
e won't tear us apart.

41, colt-less, educated,
cessful, attractive,
ght/weight proportionate,
althy.

e put on our capes and
vls and team up for ad-
ture! To the Batpoles!
kers, Two-Faces and Cat-
man need not apply.

gle white male seeks
endly Baywatch wannabe
o knows when to turn it
and when to turn it on.
quired: mouth to mouth
uscitation.

rly 20's woman looking
a gothic man who has ar
ling for the darker things

able foundation and at-
ctive appearance add to
quality and charm. Pre-
alify: you are handsome,
, 33-41, financially, emo
nally and physically fit,
to appreciate!

collector's item, low main
ance and some assembly
uired. Act now, and re-
ve a boomerang demon-
ation free! Hurry! Offer
ited.

VM, 28, tall, slender
lings (brown/blue color
eme). Safe for outdoor
d athletic use. Many
sehold uses in garden,
rkshop, kitchen. Travel
dy (extensively field
ted overseas).

year oldprofessional
king for match who's 25
handsome, honest, ma-
e and not looking for
nporary source of heat.

s GWF, 29, avid swimmer
dding private investigator
cer, is fishing for a
man who isn't afraid of
deep end.

1949 or 1953. Better like
dogs.
Get your hands dirty with
this hot young archaeologist
looking for an Indiana Jones
to excavate my secret pas-
sageways. Must have a mind

animated cuddlers to liber-
ate with in the 100 Acre
Woods of life.
SM interested in meeting an
individual who can surprise
me with her unique and of-
fensive beauties, not her ex-

graduate student, 31. Me:
postmodern hipster, English-
Literature degree, rockabilly,
like waffles. You: must hate
hippies, drunks, frozen yo-
gurt. Cat: black.
Dashing, 31, 6'3", 180lbs,

ourceful repartees
ot hype. Me,yes, flick
tr', tune whistlin', nat
flavorful, savvy, funky
jankle.
Consider dating me! E
woman I've dated in t
ve years has ended up
r former boyfriend!
lls! References avail

50 Meaningful relati
th cute dyl e who ca
ir Ford pick-up truc

mmask, join hands, ju
own, spin around, plu
to the pool? Ecstati
rpoises? I say we do

WM, 5'10", 200 pou
ack hair, eyes. Seekii
nall, all redhead, you
ney. I want the bubt
coated for us with f
ways.

ose men who cuddle
nores for love are se
their darling's char
only have tired arms
aving hugged the clo
ove.

n the prowl for a mal
ot a male line) who's
ite male, 5'7"+, 25-

WM, 36, seeking pre
ung SWF, sweetheal
eed your patien. My
ll keep you bloomin

etite white professio
ile, 45, nonsmoking
runette beauty searcl
r lion king. Scratchii
ting – all possible. L
a kill, dance all nig
nt all day.

are Virgin seeks mat
w for warm harmor
counters. Fretwork
des exceptional dra
een eyes, auburn ha
rument produces me
b, intelligent, witty a

njoys shape shifting
ssible. Blood type t
portant. Must like dra
spending some evenin
one.

ser-friendly, softwar
ized for a romantic
term relationship. Pro

UH?!?

Codex Cardiac—All the weather is for you, all the stars. All the embers sparkling in the fire, all the whiskey burning in my mouth. Your tongue would burn so much brighter.

Friendship, Companionship, Partnership—Many communionships . . . Hearth Starlight Inspiration upon the Watershed-Worship. Invocation unto Ionic-wave sensation embrace. I am AIDS recouper, 40; "negative" accommodation / "positive" vile-ability transformation "ECHO" unto Reactivity-athon. Can we you I darkman create dimensional tryst.

Many ask for modesty, yet give those who drew about themselves a chance while passing me by; many wouldn't know sincerity if Mohammed slapped them in the face. SM interested in meeting an individual who can surprise me with her unique and offensive beauties, not her extreme and unaccountable inequities.

On the Line Below—Seeking punctuation and sampling never to funny, never to much, trees, rhythmical, lyrical, black magical well designed loud strong and discriminating analog digital bedlam by the sea nymph or pretty polynomial sought by differentiable integral transformable 6′ lean (30's) impish SPM for complex variable.

"DON'T BE SHY / JUST REPLY / NICE GUY": Poems

Oh sweet young maiden, pure
and chaste

Let not thy beauty go to waste.

I'll marry thee with pomp and feast,

Without the blood of fowl, fish, or beast.

Thy smile shall spur my soul's release.

Sleeping Single in a double bed?

Want a friend and not
to get wed?

In my mid 40s, a widow
and white

For Dancing/Dining
under moonlight

If you're a Man who enjoys
the same

Give me Info and your name!

Afro-American M, 30,
very mature, nice,
good-looking.

Roses are red

Violets are blue

I'm seeking a heavy-set
female

Age 24 to 32.

In this ad, I must be truthful

49, but kinda youthful

Love kisses by the kissing
booth, jazz and friends and
the great outdoors

Walks along the quiet shores

(I hope you find my poem
useful.)

I have a little tummy
I hope that you don't mind.
I'd Rollerblade and exercise, but
I'm just not that kind.
My skin is smooth
My stature tall
My hair fall out?
No, not at all!
My face is young,
My body strong,
My arms around you,
Can't go wrong!
All is not perfect
But as you can see
If perfection's desired
You'd miss meeting me!

*Creative handsome
SWM, 37, fit and witty*

*Seeks SW/AF, 30–40,
petite and pretty*

So if you're funny-n-sweet

Call so we can meet.

Surrounding column fragments:

dust off my cover and run her fingers through my pages.

Coach—under 50, conscious, considerate, honest, patient, into snuggling, sailing. Spirited at challenging ladies. Call for tryouts.

that glimmering star to capture me in her gravitational pull. One star planet, will orbit you with affection, his molten core will fuel those passions to keep your sparkle shining.

I'm your candidate for

sense of humor, Wort's strength, Riker's height, Geordi's intelligence and communicator skills like Picard. I am shapely like Troi.

Robert DeNiro kinda guy. Seeks woman with Greenwich Village cool. Little

resourceful repartee, not hype. Me, yes, flick in', tune whistlin', nav flavorful, savvy, funky junkie.

Consider dating me! woman I've dated in the years has ended u former boyfriend's als! References avail

ar God, send me an angel we won't tear us apart.

n 41, colt-less, educated, ccessful, attractive, light/weight proportionate althy.

et's put on our capes and wls and team up for adventure! To the Batpoles! kers, Two-Faces and Catoman need not apply.

male white male seeks endly Baywatch wannabe to knows when to turn it if and when to turn it on. equired: mouth to mouth suscitation.

arly 20's woman looking r a gothic man who has an ckling for the darker things

able foundation and attractive appearance add to e quality and charm. Prealify: you are handsome, +, 33-41, financially, emonally and physically fit, e to appreciate!

collector's item, low maintenance and some assembly quired. Act now, and revive a boomerang demonstration free! Hurry! Offer mited.

WM, 28, tall, slender rlings (brown/blue color hem). Safe for outdoor d athletic use. Many usehold uses in garden, rkshop, kitchen. Travel ady (extensively field sted overseas).

0 year old professional oking for match who's 25 0, handsome, honest, mae and not looking for mporary source of heat.

his GWF, 29, avid swimmer adding private investigator, ncer, is fishing for a man who isn't afraid of e deep end.

SO Meaningful relat th cute dyke who c ir Ford pick-up tru

nmask, join hands, j wn, spin around, pl o the pool? Ecstat rpoises? I say we ev

WM, 5'10", 200 po ack hair, eyes. Seek all, all redhead, yo ney, I want the bub coated for us with ways.

ose men who cuddl ores for love are se their darling's cha nly have tired arm ving hugged the clo ove.

the prowl for a ma ot a male line) who ite male, 5'7"+, 25

WM, 36, seeking pr ung SWF, sweethea eed your pollen. My il keep you bloomin

etite white professio le, 45, nonsmoking unette beauty searc lion king. Scratch ing— all possible. I a kill, dance all nit nt all day.

are Violin seeks ma w for warm harmo counters. Fretwork des exceptional cu een eyes, auburn ha rument produces m s, intelligent, witty

njoys shape shifting rostbite. Blood type ortant. Must like dr spending some evenin alone.

User-friendly, softwa rized for a romantic rm relationship. Pre

1949 or 1955. Better like dous.

Get your hands dirty with this hot young archaeologist looking for an Indiana Jones to excavate my secret passageways. Must have a mind

animated cuddlers to hibernate with in the 100 Acre Woods of life.

SM interested in meeting an individual who can surprise me with her unique and offensive beauties, not her ex-

graduate student, 31. Me: postmodern hipster, English-Literature degree, rockabilly, like waffles. You: must hate hippies, drunks, frozen yogurt. Cat: black.

Dashing, 31, 6'3", 180lbs,

Riders on the storm

Not relating to social norms

Like a child with a home

Let's not be alone

Call me; pass the phone

Leave a number; not the tone.

GWF enjoyable to be around

etc. etc., ISO GF friends.

AKA California Girl

I work and study, work out and play

Ready for a match to make my day

He's tall (6′+) & witty, fun
& handsome

Wins my admiration, keeps
my attention,

Great conversation, ice cream
& wine

A PSWM like this sounds so fine

GOOD LUCK . . .

Seeks one-of-a-kind counterpart

Please be "normal" yet interesting

Please be working artist and financially secure

You must be bohemian at heart but with a good day job.

Prefer non-Californian [ad placed in California]

GWM, 23 y.o., ungay gay looking for another gay who is unlike other gays

---

Wants to meet a sensible young female that likes to ride on motorcycles

---

I want a woman who would not normally respond to a personal ad.

Like people for who they are and not what they look like. Have to be 5′ 8″–6′ 5″, 150–250 pounds

---

[I want] someone who knows how to cook like my Mom, cousins, and aunts.

Woman of color, seeks man color-free

SBF, mother of 1, seeking certain caliber of man. He must be sane, sober, and sincere. He must also be born Oct 25, Oct 29, Nov 2nd, Nov 11, Nov 16, or Nov 20 in the year 1958. No exceptions.

Please No . . .

Politics and Current Affairs

No political maniacs

No hardcore feminists—men hurt too

No relations to the Unabomber

No pop culture!

No guilty liberals

Please don't be a CEO who has downsized thousands of workers

Great No-Combos

No New Age flakes or left wing wackos

No CEOs, real estate agents, or Raiders fans

No Republicans or 12 steppers

No smokers or post-modernists

No Republicans or Trekkie-types!

No plumbers, lawyers need respond

No Mormons or people with 15 cats

No rednecks or crystal crunchers

No MBAs or Aquarians please

No New Age nuts, vegetarians, or Molly Ivins wanna-bes

No waiting games, pagers, or junkies

No suntanned bodybuilders or church-going easterners

Arts

No line dancers

No Dilberts!

No fear of the "arts"

No corpulent disco divas with 'tude

No violent movies

No web-heads

No Descartes please

Shouldn't steal my stereo

Sports

If 21" arms intimidate you, please don't respond

No NASCAR

No gonzo mountain bikers

Grooming

No ball caps indoors

No comb-overs

No big hair, I'm trying to quit

No butchy bad haircuts

No hair spray, please!

Sorry, dislike goatees

No pinkie rings please

No Polo wearing geeks

No artificial body parts

Spiritual No-Nos

No New Age mumbo jumbo

No Geminis

No born agains

No astrology idiots

No Bible thumpers

Behavior Problems

If you are "Americanized," please don't respond

No angries

Please do not respond if you still call your ex-girlfriend 3 times a day

No picky eaters

No lurid past please

No freaks

No mental problems

No smoking/drinking/Prozac

No 34 cases of beer every night

Coors drinkers need not apply

Don't be drunk!

Some Random No-Nos

Can't take no jive!

Please don't have a computer

Please no beepers

No engineers please

No good ol' boys

No toxic in-laws

No spouse pets

No Bob's need apply

Please no confusion

A THROUGH Z

A–Z—Adventure, balance, curious, dancing, excitement, fun, giving, happy, intimate, joyful, kind, laughter, maverick, nature, optimistic, physical, quick, romantic, sensual, talking, ultimate, variety, water, x, youthful, Zorba, 47+.

God, send me an angel won't tear us apart.

41, colt-less, educated, essfull, attractive, ht/weight proportionate thy.

s put on our capes and s and team up for ad- ure! To the Batpoles! rs, Two-Faces and Cat-- need not apply.

le white male seeks dly Baywatch wannabe knows when to turn it nd when to turn it on: ired: mouth to mouth scitation.

y 20's woman looking a gothic male who has a ng for the darker things

ole foundation and at- ive appearance add to quality and charm. Pre ify: you are handsome, 33-41, financially, emo ally and physically fit, o appreciate!

llector's item, low mai nce and some assembly ired. Act now, and re- a boomerang demon tion free! Hurry! Offer ted.

M, 28, tall, slender ngs (brown/blue color me). Safe for outdoor athletic use. Many ehold uses in garden, kshop, kitchen. Travel y (extensively field ed overseas).

year old professional ing for match who's 25 handsome, honest, ma- and not looking for porary source of heat

GWF, 29, avid swimmer ding private investigator er, is fishing for a an who isn't afraid of

proportionate F to blow the dust off my cover and run her fingers through my pages.

Coach—under 50, conscious, considerate, honest, patient, into snuggling, sailing. Spir- ited at challenging ladies. Call for tryouts.

through space, searching for that glimmering star to cap- ture me in her gravitational pull. One star planet, will orbit you with affection, his molten core will fuel those passions to keep your sparkle shining.

I'm your candidate for

1949 or 1953. Better like dogs.

Get your hands dirty with this hot young archaeologist looking for an Indiana Jones to excavate my secret pas

animated cuddlers to hiber- nate with in the 100 Acre Woods of life.

SM interested in meeting an individual who can surprise me with her unique and of-

sional WM with Data's sense of humor, Worf's strength, Riker's height, Geordi's intelligence and communicator skills like Pi- card. I am shapely like Troi.

Robert DeNiro kinda guy. Seeks woman with Green- wich Village cool. Little

graduate student, 31. Me: postmodern hipster, English- Literature degree, rockabilly, like waffles. You: must hate hippies, drunks, frozen yo- gurt. Cat: black.

hysique, enigmatic and resourceful repartees, h- not hype. Me, yes, Rick s- tin", tune whistlin", natu- flavorful, savvy, funky, to- Junkie.

Consider dating me! Ev woman I've dated in the e years has ended up r former boyfriend! N- lls! References availa

50 Meaningful relation th cute dyke who can ir Ford pick-up truck

nmask, join hands, jum own, spin around, plun to the pool? Ecstatic rpoises? I say we do

WM, 5'10", 200 pour ick hair, eyes. Seeking hall, all redhead, youn ney. I want the bubble coated for us with ho lways.

ose men who cuddle hores for love are sed their darling's charm nly have tired arms f ving hugged the cloud ove.

n the prowl for a male t a male line) who's ite male, 5'7"+, 25-4

WM, 36, seeking pret ung SWF, sweetheart eed your pollen. My si ll keep you blooming.

tite white profession ale, 45, nonsmoking onette beauty search r Ellin King. Scratchin ting—all possible. Le r a kill, dance all nigh ut all day.

re Violin seeks match w for warm harmoni counters. Fretwork in udes exceptional curv een eyes, auburn hair rument produces mel s, intelligent, witty so

njoys shape shifting a ostbite. Blood type un ortant. Must like drag ending some evening one.

ser-friendly, software nized for a romantic, lo

Academia and Alanis, bagels, caring, DC fan, embracing, fairness, guttermouth, Hotel New Hampshire, insightful, Jewish, k. d. lang, laughter, malapropism, New York, openness, partnership, quick-witted, robust coffee, silly, teacher, uh duh, voguish stuff, watching *Annie Hall*, x goes here, youthful, zoom lens, ISO SJF, with A to Z, 25–35 y.o., educated, creative, independent, and likes to laugh her tush off.

Z THROUGH A

Alphabet Soup—Zest, yearning, exploring, *Wind in the Willows*, verbal, unique, travel, Scrabble, roses, quixotic, pomegranates, olive oil, Neruda, music and math, languages, Klimt, jingles, eyes, hills, gentle, forties, enthusiastic, dancing, compassion, blond and blue, available! Partnering with parenting prospects appeals, letters warmly welcome!

AD POSSIBLY EXAGGERATED

American hero leaps tall buildings in single bound, more powerful than locomotive, toothpaste ads feature my smile, leading tailors copy my style, design suspension bridges in spare time, settle revolutions in Spain while on vacation, Touchstone and MGM have asked me to star, condo with a view, but I haven't met you. ISO special lady, N/S, W or AF, 25–40 years, beautiful, fit, and trim.

Don't respond to this ad . . .
unless you're interested in meeting a SWM, 42, 5′ 11″, Olympic medalist, rock and roll star, rocket scientist, CIA spy, thirteenth man to walk on the moon, climbed Mount Everest, invented Tupperware and fuel injection. You: SWF, 30–42, attractive, slender, degreed professional with a great sense of humor and similar resume.

SWPM, 36, with a warthog's face, walrus' physique, drunken rhino's disposition. Slovenly appearance, sloth-like motivation, and illiterate to a fault. I'll be financially secure once I sue the owner of the toxic waste dump where my pop-up camper rests. I'd like to meet an intelligent, caring, humorous, attractive 27–44 year old woman.

DATE ME, I'M FUNNY

Seeking clone of last girlfriend (as she was of the one before her) to help me re-enact lifetime of co-dependent behavior. SWM, 38, hair, eyes, etc.

SWF, 50ish. I am post-menopausal and I have cellulite. I am an old maid who reads the obituary column first. I channel a 35,000 year old spirit named Louis. I can get you in touch with all your dead musician and music industry friends.

I have a puppy. He's the sweetest little puppy. Soft and fluffy. Big brown eyes. He has a little puppy tongue and puppy breath, and he knows how to give Eskimo kisses. When he plays under the blankets or shirts from the laundry and he pokes his head out, it's the cutest thing you ever saw. If you want him to live, call me.

Name the Cat. His name is switched every year to keep him properly befuddled. Pick the 1999 nom de guerre (previously: Malice, Pernicious, Xeng Xhi Shek) and win a date with graduate student, 31. Me: postmodern hipster, English Literature degree, rockabilly, like waffles. You: must hate hippies, drunks, frozen yogurt. Cat: black.

ISO Bad Ass Superfreak. Don't have to be a superstar. Should be tough and cool, semi-sarcastic, roll in the gutter but clean up well (not my dishes or laundry). Me: punk-hipster-doofus, studying and working, prodigal with food and drink, yet athletic like Jack LaLanne, 5′ 8″, decongested, 29 years old, aerodynamic, 160 lbs.

You, no, wind-up, tabacky usin',
permanent depressed, budget
bimbo, hump me dump me, rocket
ranger. Yes mental muscle, proud
physique, enigmatic anima,
resourceful repartees, hip not
hype. Me, no, puff pastried, cross
bearing, freeze dried, bachelor
breeder bugle boy. Yes, flick sittin',
tune whistlin', naturally flavorful,
savvy, funky, travel junkie.

Wanted—Mel Tormé disco records, left-handed canoe, new or used Chia Pets, anything with the image of cheese printed on it, bowling shoes, bowling hats, bowling trusses, 1750 Immanuel Kant rookie card. Also need girlfriend. No calls before 7:00 a.m.

DATE AT YOUR OWN RISK

Charismatic fast talker seeks lawyer to arrange my staff, guarantee my investments, and ignore my many infidelities. The perfect woman.

ISO Meaningful relationship with cute dyke who can repair Ford pick-up truck. Must have own tools and transportation.

Top left column:

...proportionate F to blow the dust off my cover and run her fingers through my pages.

Coach—under 50, conscious, considerate, honest, patient, into snuggling, sailing. Spirited at challenging ladies. Call for tryouts.

Top second column:

...through space, searching for that glimmering star to capture me in her gravitational pull. One star planet, will orbit you with affection, his molten core will fuel those passions to keep your sparkle shining.

I'm your candidate for...

Top third column:

...sional WM with Data's sense of humor, Worf's strength, Riker's height, Geordi's intelligence and communicator skills like Picard. I am shapely like Troi.

Robert DeNiro kinda guy. Seeks woman with Greenwich Village cool. Little...

Top right column:

...psique, enigmatic, and resourceful repartees, h nit hype. Me,yes, flick s tin', tune whistlin', natu flavorful, savvy, funky, tw Junkie.

Consider dating me! Ev woman I've dated in the r years has ended up r former boyfriend! N ults! References availab

Left column:

God, send me an angel, won't tear us apart.

41, colt-less, educated, essful, attractive, nt/weight proportionate, thy.

s put on our capes and s and team up for adure! To the Batpoles! rs, Two-Faces and Catman need not apply.

ale white male seeks ndly Baywatch wannabe knows when to turn it and when to turn it on. uired: mouth to mouth scitation.

y 20's woman looking a gothic man who has an ng for the darker things.

ale foundation and attve appearance add to quality and charm. Preify: you are handsome, 33-41, financially, emoally and physically fit, o appreciate!

llector's item, low mainnce and some assembly ired. Act now, and ree a boomerang demontion free! Hurry! Offer ced.

M, 28, tall, slender ngs (brown/blue color me). Safe for outdoor athletic use. Many sehold uses in garden, kshop, kitchen. Travel y (extensively held ed overseas).

year oldprofessional ing for match who's 25-handsome, honest, maand not looking for porary source of heat

GWF, 29, avid swimmer ding private investigator, er, is fishing for a nan who isn't afraid of deep end

Right column:

...hmask, join hands, jun wn, spin around, plun o the pool? Ecstatic rpoises? I say we do i

WM, 5'10", 200 pour ack hair, eyes. Seeking nall, all redhead, youn ney. I want the bubble coated for us with he ways.

ose men who cuddle nores for love are sed their darling's charm nly have tired arms f ving hugged the cloud ove.

the prowl for a mate ot a male line) who's s ite male, 5'7"+, 25-4

WM, 36, seeking prett ung SWF, sweetheart eed your pollen. My sl ll keep you blooming.

tite white professiona ale, 45, nonsmoking unette beauty searchi llon king. Scratchin ing—all possible. Le a kill, dance all nigh all day.

are Violin seeks match w for warm harmonic counters. Fretwork in udes exceptional curv en eyes, auburn hair. rument produces melo s, intelligent, witty so

njoys shape shifting a frostbite. Blood type un portant. Must like drag spending some evening a one.

User-friendly, software mized for a romantic, r

Bottom left:

...1949 or 1953. Better like dogs.

Get your hands dirty with this hot young archaeologist looking for an Indiana Jones to excavate my secret pas-

Bottom second column:

...more than hair, seeks other animated cuddlers to hibernate with in the 100 Acre Woods of life.

SM interested in meeting an individual who can surprise me with her unique and of-

Bottom third column:

...graduate student, 31. Me: postmodern hipster, English-Literature degree, rockabilly, like waffles. You: must hate hippies, drunks, frozen yogurt. Cat: black.

Ladies! Afraid of losing your man? Want to make him jealous? Consider dating me! Every woman I've dated in the last five years has ended up with her former boyfriend! Never fails! References available.

Twentieth century disease—Too many chemicals make me sick. I eat pure foods, go pristine places, and think positive thoughts as much as possible. No fragrance products, smoke, solvents tolerated. Nice, clean fun.

UNCLASSIFIABLE ADS

Torn: SWM, 30, Right leg still running to the wild side of my 20s. ISO SF to keep one leg in each world.

The Canvas . . . brushed with brilliant strokes, two masked figures appear—strangers on a ridge under ultramarine sky; steaming thermal mists rise up invitingly. Unmask, join hands, jump down, spin around, plunge into the pool? Ecstatic little porpoises? I say we do it!

seeks "rapturous" rela
ship with one bright,
y, easy to look at, easy
with SWM feathered
d [43-55].

blood—This charming,
37 seeks the perfect F
and new lover with lip
sugar, "boy meets girl"
God, send me an ange
won't tear us apart.

41, cult-less, educated,
essful, attractive,
nt/weight proportionat
thy.

put on our capes and
s and team up for ad-
ure! To the Batpoles!
rs, Two-Faces and Cat
an need not apply.

le white male seek s
dly Baywatch wannab
knows when to turn it
and when to turn it on.
ired: mouth to mouth
scitation.

y 20's woman looking
gothic man who has
ng for the darker thing

le foundation and at-
ve appearance add to
uality and charm. Pre
ty: you are handsome,
33-41, financially, emo
ally and physically fit,
appreciate!

llector's item, low ma
nce and some assembl
ired. Act now, and re-
a boomerang demon-
ion free! Hurry! Offer
ed.

M, 28, tall, slender
gs (brown/blue color
me). Safe for outdoor
athletic use. Many
ehold uses in garden,
shop, kitchen. Travel
y (extensively field
d overseas).

ear oldprofessional
ng for match who's 2
andsome, honest, ma
and not looking for
orary source of heat.

GWF, 29, avid swimm
ing private investigato
is fishing for a
an who isn't afraid of
ep end.

proportionate F to blow the
dust off my cover and run
her fingers through my
pages.

Coach—under 50, conscious,
considerate, honest, patient,
into snuggling, sailing. Spirited at challenging ladies.
Call for tryouts.

through space, searching for
that glimmering star to capture me in her gravitational
pull. One star planet, will
orbit you with affection, his
molten core will fuel those
passions to keep your
sparkle shining.

I'm your candidate for

sional WM with Data's
sense of humor, Worf's
strength, Riker's height,
Geordi's intelligence and
communicator skills like Picard. I am shapely like Troi.

Robert DeNiro kinda guy.
Seeks woman with Green-
wich Village cool. Little

All red bubble. SWM,
5′ 10″, 200 pounds,
black hair, eyes. Seeking
small, all redhead, young
honey. I want the bubble
to be coated for us with
honey always. Honey work,
play honey. When I find
you, you'll be my air
balloon always.

er former boyfriend! N
ails! References availa

50 Meaningful relation
with cute dyke who can
pair Ford pick-up truck

Unmask, join hands, jur
own, spin around, plun
nto the pool? Ecstatic
orpoises? I say we do

SWM, 5'10", 200 poun
lack hair, eyes. Seeking
mall, all redhead, youn
oney. I want the bubble
e coated for us with ho
always.

Those men who cuddle
whores for love are sed
y their darling's charm
only have tired arms f
having hugged the cloud
above.

n the prowl for a male.
not a male line) who's
white male, 5'7"+, 25-4

SWM, 36, seeking prett
young SWF, sweetheart.
Need your pollen. My st
will keep you blooming.

Petite white profession
male, 45, nonsmoking
brunette beauty searchi
or lion king. Scratching
iting – all possible. Let
or a kill, dance all night
unt all day.

are Violin seeks matchi
how for warm harmonio
ncounters. Fretwork in
ludes exceptional curve
reen eyes, auburn hair.
trument produces melo
us, intelligent, witty so

njoys shape shifting am
rostbite. Blood type im
ortant. Must like drag
pending some evening
lone.

User-friendly, software,
nized for a romantic, lo

1949 or 1953. Better like
dogs.

Get your hands dirty with
this hot young archaeologist
looking for an Indiana Jones
to excavate my secret pas-

animated cuddlers to hiber-
nate with in the 100 Acre
Woods of life.

SM interested in meeting an
individual who can surprise
me with her unique and of-

graduate student, 31. Me:
postmodern hipster, English-
Literature degree, rockabilly,
like waffles. You: must hate
hippies, drunks, frozen yo-
gurt. Cat: black.

Addictions, afflictions, affections be bi beau brew concerts computers connections construction laughter lizards music memories madness movies patient persistent persuasive remodeling relaxing rock space taping tipping tripping play the home game take the taste test call.

Those men who cuddle whores for love are sedated by their darling's charms but I only have tired arms from having hugged the clouds above.

dust off my cover and run her fingers through my pages.

Coach—under 50, conscious, considerate, honest, patient, into snuggling, sailing. Spirited at challenging ladies.

that glimmering star to capture me in her gravitational pull. One star planet, will orbit you with affection, his molten core will fuel those passions to keep your sparkle shining.

sense of humor, Worf's strength, Riker's height, Geordi's intelligence and communicator skills like Picard. I am shapely like Troi.

Robert DeNiro kinda guy. Seeks woman with Green-

Kiss me Guido. 31 year old Italian-American, 6′, 225 lbs., Tauran, pasta cookin', canoli eatin', Botticelli lovin', Italian speakin', Fellini watchin', Armani wearin', garlic fanatic seeks Mr. Wonderful under 40 for romance. Ciao bello.

1949 or 1953. Better like dogs.

Get your hands dirty with this hot young archaeologist looking for an Indiana Jones to excavate my secret pas-

animated cuddlers to hibernate with in the 100 Acre Woods of life.

SM interested in meeting an individual who can surprise me with her unique and of-

graduate student, 31. Me: postmodern hipster, English-Literature degree, rockabilly, like waffles. You: must hate hippies, drunks, frozen yogurt. Cat: black.